Praise for *Made for More*

"Lindsay wants us to move from confusion to clarity, and this is **a masterful guide**. I found myself breathing slowly, paying attention to my body, and feeling empowered to stop and try her ideas or answer her questions. I can see this being a book with all the dog-eared pages and coffee stains because of its daily applicable advice."
—**Amy Seiffert,** author of *Grace Looks Amazing on You*

"**Inspiring, thought-provoking, and relatable.** In a world so busy with to-do lists and digital distractions, Lindsay breaks down the beliefs and barriers that hold many of us back. Her strategies and stories offer readers practical ways to release these old habits and live a life that truly fuels them."
—**Dr. Nicole Clement, ND,** Skin Method

"This book has such **impact potential for next-generation world-changers**—to be able to step into their own, and take ownership and radical responsibility over their happiness, their potential, and their impact on this world."
—**Dr. Erin TeWinkel, ND,** cofounder of The Teen Collective

"*Made for More* provides **unique tools and inspiration for young women of today**, and reminds us all to approach life with an open mind, always creating space for what you truly want to do."
—**Marci Cooper,** founder of Sage Solstice Wellness

"As a mom, mother-in-law, and co-worker to this generation, I love *Made for More*'s **artful encouragement of our Gen Z women** to be free of society and internal constraints and to find happiness in their own way. I think we could all use 'more strolling and less scrolling'!"
—**Tara Bevington,** president, Vancouver Island Association of Women Police

"This book is like a love letter to every woman's younger self."
—**Lisa Charleyboy,** editor, *Not Your Pocahontas*

ALSO BY LINDSAY SEALEY

5 Ways to Become Even Stronger

A-Z Self-Care

Finding Your Way

Girls Can Do Hard Things

Growing Girl Champions

Growing Girls

Growing Strong Girls: Practical Tools to Cultivate Connection in the Preteen Years

Growing Teenage Girls

How to Help Her

Rooted, Resilient, and Ready: Empowering Teen Girls as They Grow

Smart and Scattered … Now What?

True Beauty

Visit LindsaySealey.com for additional ebooks, handouts, blog posts, products, and the enhancements for this book.

A FRESH START
APPROACH TO A
Bolder, Brighter You

Lindsay Sealey, MA Ed

Foreword by Delia Perry

Copyright © 2022 by Lindsay Sealey
Foreword copyright © 2022 by Delia Perry

22 23 24 25 26   5 4 3 2 1

All rights reserved. No part of this book may be reproduced, stored in a retrieval system or transmitted, in any form or by any means, without the prior written consent of the publisher.

Library of Congress Control Number: 2021923599

ISBN 978-1-63756-006-8 (paperback)
ISBN 978-1-63756-007-5 (EPUB)

Editor: Sarah Brohman
Cover design and interior design: Morgan Krehbiel
Author photo: Melanie Tocher of Belly Baby & Beyond Photography
@bellybabybeyondphotography

Published by Wonderwell in Los Angeles, CA
www.wonderwell.press

Distributed in the US by Publishers Group West and
in Canada by Publishers Group Canada

Printed and bound in China

A fresh start is not just important, it is necessary, and you deserve a chance to begin again, every single day.

Contents

Foreword • *ix*

A Fresh Start World • *1*
Creating a More and Less Life • *11*
Letter from Lindsay • *15*

CHAPTER 1 • *17*
More Happiness, Less Waiting

CHAPTER 2 • *43*
More Confidence, Less Doubt

CHAPTER 3 • *73*
More Authenticity, Less Conformity

CHAPTER 4 • *101*
More Progress, Less Perfection

CHAPTER 5 • *129*
More Mindfulness, Less Distraction

CHAPTER 6 • *159*
More Connection, Less Separation

CHAPTER 7 • *191*
More Power, Less Fear

Letter to Yourself • *220*
Last Thoughts • *223*

Acknowledgments • *224*
Notes • *226*
Bibliography • *228*
About the Author • *229*

Foreword

Like many of you, there are days when I seek inspiration from Instagram. I am feeling I need something to get me excited and help me feel hopeful and positive. That's why August 16, 2019, though it started off like any other day, was an important memory for me.

Yes, it is likely I woke up at the crack of dawn to get a workout in, read something uplifting, and spend a little time reflecting on my day ahead before I had to hit the ground running as a busy mom of two. I am also pretty sure that, at some point that same morning, I took a few moments to scroll through my Instagram feed. No, I wasn't expecting what I found.

As I scrolled looking for that "something more," I ran across an account called @boldnewgirls. I was immediately drawn in by the bright and eye-catching photos, but even more so by the uplifting messages contained in the posts about confidence, bravery, and power. I immediately felt like whoever the author of the content was shared the same deep desire I had, which was to empower women to live their best lives.

I immediately decided to send a private message simply to say how much I appreciated what they were doing to inspire others, especially girls. That set off a chain of messages and conversations between Lindsay Sealey and me. Those chats led to Lindsay becoming a two-time guest on my podcast, *Girls 4 Greatness*, for her books *Growing Strong Girls* and *Rooted, Resilient, and Ready*, and most importantly, it led to the start of a wonderful friendship.

Over the last three years, I have closely followed Lindsay and all the amazing things she is doing with her Bold New Girls community. I have read her books, seen her shine on live media interviews, listened to her podcast interviews, enjoyed her blogs, programs, and courses, and watched her YouTube channel. Lindsay is an incredibly talented communicator and writer because of not just the wealth of knowledge she shares but also the way in which she delivers that knowledge. This book is yet another beautiful example of how Lindsay deeply and genuinely cares for others, particularly the young women she is so passionate and relentless about championing.

Made for More is a book that will challenge anyone to examine how they can bring more of what they want into their life and leave behind those things that are no longer serving them. This is a call to action for young women to let go of pressure, perfection, and the need to prove themselves and to look toward acceptance, incremental change, and the process of pursuing purpose.

I have interviewed nearly one hundred and fifty women on my podcast throughout the last four years. Each of these women has overcome great struggles and obstacles to impact the world in their own unique, powerful way. I firmly believe that these women would not be the influencers they are if they did not have to wrestle with letting go of something to bring more of what they did want into their lives. They all seem to know that good stories take time to write and that there is no "instant" or Amazon Prime when it comes to their stories.

In this book, Lindsay's honest, carefully thought-out words serve as an incredible reminder to wake up and embrace the one life we have been given. Her words also offer hope as she reminds us that we have it in our power to craft the life each of us wants to be living and that we can also utilize that power at any given moment. Or as Lindsay writes, "Every day you can choose to change your mind, your priorities, and your lifestyle."

You are about to embark on a wonderful journey of self-discovery with Lindsay. This book, encouraging you to step into your truth, will pave the way and help anyone who finds themselves at a crossroads in life or at a point in which they are wanting to make a change but just don't know where to begin. The essence of Lindsay's creation is this: meet yourself where you are at—even if it's in the middle of your mess, even if you don't feel worthy or ready for any change—then decide what your lifestyle of more and less could be.

I have no doubt that this book will challenge you and motivate you to change, as you stop thinking you are not worthy of the work it takes to make change happen and you start to truly believe you are meant for *greatness*. Like I often say at the end of each episode of my podcast, Lindsay will remind you that you are indeed worthy of living the life *you* really and truly were meant to live.

—Delia Perry, host of *Girls 4 Greatness* podcast

A Fresh Start World

Liv came to see me at the end of last summer. She walked tall and confidently into my workspace wearing a bright-green cropped sweater and white low-rise jeans, her nails neatly manicured, her long dark hair perfectly straightened. I could tell her outfit was planned out and thoughtful. I could also tell something was wrong. Liv didn't look sad exactly—she looked serious, as though something deep was on her mind. When I asked her why she came to see me now, at the age of twenty-one, she told me this: "I graduated high school four years ago, and although I wanted a gap year, I went to college. I did a little partying, a lot of studying, and I just earned my liberal arts degree. People joke about earning a degree and then working at Starbucks, and now that's exactly what I'm doing. I moved back home with my mom and my younger brothers, and I feel my plan to go to school is finished. But I don't have any new plans. I'm wondering and worrying about my what's next."

Liv's experience is not uncommon. Many young women come to see me when they reach a place where their plan is completed or needs tweaking or even a fresh start. Maybe you need a fresh start, too?

Liv and I worked together for several months on a tool I created called Rainbow Thinking. This tool is a chance to brainstorm all ideas and possibilities and to take time to explore what fits and feels best for clients. The rainbow is a symbol of hope and optimism based on the belief that anything can happen, and it all begins with imagining, asking "what if?"

Liv did continue to work at the coffee shop. She also tried nannying and accompanied one family to Italy for a month. She applied to a lot of different jobs and waited to hear back from employers. Her year was filled with taking chances and trying new things, so I wasn't surprised that, when she got a call from a movie company for a job editing scripts, she immediately said yes.

If you ask Liv if this was her plan, she'd tell you no. But she'd also tell you that by having an open mind and heart, trying lots of different options, and working hard, this new plan that she's now living is even better than she could have imagined! She simultaneously learned how to get more comfortable with not knowing the plan and realized that she had the power to create a new plan. Guess what? Liv started to look happier and more confident!

For more than twenty years now, I have been an educator, consultant, speaker, and author, and I have loved every part of my journey. With three internationally published books, a speaking career, and a pretty happy and balanced life, I am confident in my ability to encourage, advocate for, and be a cheerleader and champion for young women, like you. I know that the era of young adulthood is full of ups and downs, mistakes and failures, and new things. I also know you can make a fresh start any time with a go-for-it attitude, some helpful tips and tricks, and ongoing support.

When I began my company, Bold New Girls, I was teaching and coaching young girls. I now teach teen girls and young women just like Liv, and their parents as well. This shift in my client base happened naturally as my younger clients grew up and headed out into the "real world." As they did, I started to notice that there were expectations—placed upon them by others and themselves—that they should know how to adult without necessarily learning how or having the tools to do so. As they realized their choices were endless, so too was their stress and anxiety. Of course, the gap that I could see motivated me to support my clients in new ways and to be with them as they grew into young and capable women.

Today, I meet with a lot of young women who struggle, get caught in a rut, and feel they don't know where to turn to. That may not be you right now, but that doesn't mean that you won't need some support and encouragement in the future when you are feeling low or would like to learn some skills that can help you grow into your adulthood.

My "job," which is my passion and privilege, is to show up for young women, wherever they are, to hold space for them, to reflect back to them their strengths and talents, to encourage them when they need it most, to remind them just how strong they can be, to be curious about their ideas and thoughts. I believe in them, and I know that they are trying and can create the lives they really want. I meet young women on bad days when they feel like giving up, during times they are disappointed, frustrated, or have lost hope, and when they feel they simply "can't." But I also meet them in moments of triumph, like when they get the job they've been working toward, when they earn the contract they've been hustling for, when they find someone they want to be with, when they are doing the hard things and realizing their dreams are happening.

I tell my clients repeatedly, "I'll talk about anything with you," and we do! We talk about everything from food, fitness, and cycle syncing to breakups, makeups, and cultivating connections. We explore the pressures they feel to be perfect Super Women, the worries they have about not meeting their own expectations or disappointing family and friends. We talk about their feelings of loneliness and isolation as with their need to fit and belong, their fears about what they'll do and their future, their desire to accept and love themselves and find mutual love. We dive deep into their struggles when it comes to confidence, feeling good enough, setting boundaries, and speaking up, as well as their need to discover their place and purpose and make a difference. All the while, they are wondering "what now?" and "what's next?"

I have noticed, as I am sure you have, that the world has really changed—even since a year ago when I was writing this book. Amid the countless natural disasters and climate change, a global pandemic, growing social movements such as #blacklivesmatter (BLM), #metoo, and #timesup, the plight of the Indigenous peoples and #everychildmatters, #stopasianhate, political unrest, and economic devastation, the world has been shocked into disbelief and lockdown. Many of us struggle to make new plans or pay our rent, much less make sense of our new upside-down world. But I believe that we are being called to change. As life unfolds and seems to get more challenging each day, we wait for times when things might be even better. New ideas, innovative solutions, and remote everything shows us that life is changing, for the better. I want to encourage you to move beyond observing the changes to become part of the changes.

Here's why.

The world needs you to be the next generation of healers, ceiling breakers, inventors and engineers, daredevils and designers, mentors and teachers, doctors and lawyers, superstar athletes, amazing moms, authors, innovators and influencers, environmentalists, politicians and advocates, boundary pushers and boundary defiers, leaders and luminaries, rebels with causes, and change- and difference-makers. But first, to feel your best and to show up with self-belief and confidence, you will need to start where you are at and do this little by little, step by step.

Today, the growing individuals of Generation Z, born between 1995 and 2012, are on the move; they have more choice and challenge than ever before. As stated by the Network of Executive Women (NEW), this is a new generation, one that will surpass millennials as the largest generation and who are "about to step onto the world stage, entering the workforce and spending money on the products, services, and solutions that you produce, provide and create . . . the impact of their entry will be swift and profound."[1]

The young women of Gen Z are smart, passionate, purposeful, and powerful participants, actively involved in social movements from climate change to women's rights. Gen Z women are creating and standing upon platforms, making their voices heard, and promoting real change. They are fast becoming fierce and fearless ceiling breakers. They are "woke"—alert and aware of cultural changes and social injustices—and ready to take on new perspective in the workplace and redefine success.

Gen Z is also known as the competitive generation, one that arrives in a disruptive decade of increasing change and complexity. This era is defined by its lack of definition as well as fluidity with respect to clear roles, traditions, expectations, family life, and social and political influences. All of this is embedded in a pervasive, inescapable digital layer to life. The youth of Gen Z have never known another way apart from defying the norm.[2]

Yet, even with seemingly endless opportunities found instantly in a Google search, the young women of Generation Z sometimes feel too busy, too tired, too fearful, and overwhelmed by too much information. They are easily caught up in stagnation or in the vortex of perfectionism and procrastination. The Super Girls of the teen years become the Super Women of young adulthood, trying to be all things to all people. Although they are accused of being selfie—and social media—obsessed, incessantly posting and swiping, or lazy, entitled, and even complacent, in reality they feel tremendous pressure to be successful in a world that is rapidly changing—economically, socially, and politically—as they contend with their own changing beliefs and ideas, social circles, and priorities. Life can feel difficult, uncomfortable, and complicated.

Does this sound like you or reflect how you are feeling?

Grown-ish is likely the best word I can use to describe how you might be feeling in this phase of your life. You are not growing up as quickly or as intensely as you did when you were a young girl, becoming a tween and then a teenager, but maybe you feel not yet grown enough to consider yourself an adult. Where you are right now is a season of sorting, experimenting, and becoming.

You are in flux as you dig deep into who you are and what is next for you. You may be making multiple transitions: leaving high school and going to college, moving out of your family home, taking a gap year, finding your first job in your chosen career path, making new friends, getting into long-term relationships, wanting to deepen your interests and skill set, and learning new things about yourself and the world. As you are growing, it is also likely you are facing some obstacles along the way. Perhaps things that aren't working out as you thought they might. Maybe you need to explore making a fresh start.

Take a moment to reflect on these questions:

- How do you feel about yourself right now?
- How do you deal with stress and anxiety?
- Do you surround yourself with emotionally healthy people?
- Are you able to set boundaries and practice self-care?
- Do you get enough sleep, water, and nutritious food?
- Are you moving your body regularly?
- How much time do you spend scrolling through social media?
- Are you motivated to get going and growing?
- Do you feel under pressure to be "somebody" and to be "perfect"?
- Are you following your passions and doing what makes you feel most alive?
- Are you committed to personal growth and making yourself a priority?

I want to acknowledge this may feel like even more pressure. You may be thinking:

- I am too broken or messed up.
- I am too fragile or afraid.
- I am too busy.
- I am too stressed out.
- I am too distracted.
- I am too tired.
- I am not ready.

These feelings are normal and to be expected, because if you are like so many of my clients, change—a fresh start in particular—can feel scary as there is so much you don't have figured out yet. You may have ideas but not necessarily the next steps or tools to help you get started, or you may have no idea what you want. Of course, I understand that there are many variables in your life experiences. Even the most confident young women who are excited about the future will have their trying times, times when they are filled with wonder and worry about tomorrow.

Made for More explores many of the concerns and questions you may have about this phase of your life. This book is an all-inclusive experience infused with stories, ideas, examples, powerful affirmations, check-in questions for reflection, and practical, relevant ways for you to design your days and, yes, your dreams. Together, we will explore seven pivotal areas of growth, including:

- Happiness
- Confidence
- Authenticity
- Progression
- Mindfulness
- Connection
- Power

My goal is to help you become a stronger, happier, healthier, more confident, and more secure you who knows and shows their value and worth. I hope this book will help you make your fresh start!

Every day is an opportunity to start fresh—to let go of your yesterday and to create an even better today with even more bravery, confidence, happiness, and self-belief. Every day you can choose to change your mind, your priorities, and your lifestyle. Yet, a fresh start isn't about simply changing your mind or figuring out what's next in the aftermath of disaster. It is your positive and proactive approach to creating new opportunities and living your best life in this unique time. Fresh starts aren't someday or even one-day ideas—they are actions you can take today.

Today you can start again. You can start again every day. It's okay to make mistakes and go through times of stagnation. Focus on one step, one day at a time, and keep going. Choosing to make a fresh start is your choice, and you can do this as much and as often as you need. You may want a fresh idea or mindset, fresh and healthy habits or lifestyle changes, or fresh inspiration and opportunities. For example, a fresh start for you might mean:

- A fresh pair of pajamas and new bedding
- A fresh workout routine
- A fresh nutrition plan
- A fresh attitude when it comes to work or school
- A fresh way to look at your old belief systems or set boundaries
- A fresh activity
- A fresh take on what you really want to do next
- A fresh plan or approach to how you live your life

No matter where you are and what's happening for you, believe me when I say you deserve a fresh start. This book will not only explain how necessary this is but also explore all the ways you can do this. Maybe you think you're too young to be thinking about fresh starts, since you're only just beginning your adulthood. But we all need permission to have a fresh start every day. At times in my life, a fresh start is exactly what I needed.

When I was in my early twenties, I began my career as a teacher. It was my fresh start after years of schooling, and I was ready! Although at first I loved this career experience, eventually I had to face the truth: I had outgrown my position. I kept thinking that I should be thankful; this is a good job and a good life. This thought kept me going for a while, then the little voice inside of me would speak up again, encouraging me to stop living someone else's dream and start creating dreams of my own. So, I did what I always knew to do: I started creating.

In any spare moment, I started to moonlight—the practice of working a second job outside normal business hours. I would pour my ideas into my binder of possibilities. I imagined in detail what my company would be like from the logo and website to my ideal clients, what curriculum I'd teach, and even what I'd charge. Interestingly, I wasn't ready to quit my teaching day job at the time because I couldn't possibly imagine leaving it. Yet over time, leaving became inevitable. The desire to see what would happen and to take the chance soon outweighed the worry of failing.

Quitting was the hardest thing I've ever done. Staying would have been easier, but I knew it would not feel better. Understanding that felt both incredibly freeing and incredibly terrifying. I let go of the comfort and security of a regular paycheck, along with familiar routines and predictable days, to venture into a less predictable opportunity on my own.

My job was an ending (that couldn't have gone worse; I'll talk more about that in the last chapter of this book) as much as it was a beginning (that couldn't have gone better). You know what? As difficult as this transition time was for me, I have absolutely no regrets, and I wouldn't change a thing. Starting my company, Bold New Girls, was a big fresh start that came at a time of plateau in my career. My fresh start taught me this game changer: if I wanted to create more of what I wanted—working for myself—I had to do less and let go of what I didn't want—working for someone else.

This more and less approach is the fundamental tool for this book and an approach I hope you will boldly embrace. The **more and less** approach to life is about choosing to let go and leave behind what you don't want to create space for what you do want. It is your decision to ask what you want both **more** *and* **less** of and then making that fresh start. If you want more of anything, you are going to need less of something else, such as more happiness and confidence and less insecurity and self-doubt. The **more and less** platform is what will help you grow into your brightest, boldest, best self!

You are growing, changing in every way. This is the start of something new. This can be both exhilarating and scary, but I am here to help you every step of the way! After all, there is no better time for a fresh start, and I want you to feel alive, refreshed, and ready. Are you ready?

A Note to Reader

I wrote *Made for More* to encourage and empower young women and individuals who identify as female as they move from the teenage years to the ever-complicated, yet ever-enriching adult years. My aim is to offer an integration of the most relevant and up-to-date research, as well as stories and unique and diversified experiences, practical tools and techniques, ideas, and inspiration.

Simultaneously, this book needs to be inclusive in terms of race, culture, education, religion, socio-economic status, and beliefs and values as we move into greater possibilities of understanding humanity. We all benefit from becoming more thoughtful and aware, mindful and sensitive, as the world changes and as we all adapt, adjust, and change.

Since books are constrained by societal constructs of gender identification and nontraditional gender identities, the pronouns *she*, *her*, *they*, and *them* are used interchangeably throughout the book, even though individuals may align with nonbinary, genderfluid, or genderflux pronouns.

Though my goal is to be consciously aware of differences, of course I hold inevitable limitations and implicit biases. I cannot apologize for my unique life experiences and knowledge base, but I do apologize if I am unaware of ideas or information that may be important and relevant to you.

My intention would never be to offend, dismiss, or ignore what matters most to others. I have both a privilege and responsibility as a writer and as a global citizen to express myself objectively but with sensitivity and thoughtfulness.

Equally important to note is that a book can never replace professional help and support, though it can provide information and ideas. If you, or someone you know, needs medical or other professional attention, please seek customized advice and guidance.

Finally, the stories woven into this book were chosen for their uniqueness and diversity of life experiences.

Creating a More and Less Life

The inspiration for this book came to me through an unlikely trio: a sermon, an Instagram post, and a T-shirt. Here's what happened: I heard a pastor preach this message, "You are good enough, and I'm going to call you to be even better, even more." Then I saw an Instagram post by @positivelypresent with a colorful array of pictures and the caption "how to be even more happy." On the same day I found a T-shirt in a boutique store with a list of "more" suggestions such as more music, more sunsets, and more flowers.

Never one to ignore signs of serendipity, my mind began playing around with the juxtaposition of what I felt young women needed more of today. This got me thinking about one of the most powerful questions I have learned to ask myself: What if?

This simple question is packed with limitless potential and infinite possibilities. This game-changing query opens you up to wonder, dares you to dream, encourages you to consider. I have asked myself "what if?" when I need to get myself thinking, then moving forward. What if I was a little braver and a little less afraid? What if I said what I really wanted to say and stopped caring about what people think of me? Or even simpler, what if I figured out how to become more tech savvy or what if I read more books?

"What if" can be your first step as you consider what you want and how you will make it happen. As you think about what's possible, you may find that your energy and enthusiasm shift and that you start to believe that you can make change. With the power of "what if" in your mind, what if I told you that you can have more of what you want and less of what you don't want? Would you believe me? Would you be willing to try?

Made and Meant for More

You are made and meant for more. You are so much more than your yesterday; your mistakes and missteps; your academic, athletic, or career achievements; your "perfect" social media life. When you believe you deserve more, you feel confident to clarify exactly what you want and need and are more intentional about acting on those needs.

You are even more than all you have accumulated and all you have to show for your life. There is something so much more, so much better, and so much more meaningful than who you are today. You do have a purpose. Meet yourself where you are and consider this: explore the idea of bringing the approach of doing **more and less** into your life. Let me explain what I mean.

Many young women tell me how their lives are crammed with positive things like a job, relationships, volunteer work, and life goals. But, at the same time, they also hold on to self-sabotaging things, such as competing interests, emotional baggage, mistakes, and self-criticism, or they are filled with FOMO (fear of missing out). In a strange way, their busy lives sometimes cause them to feel unfulfilled. Do you feel this way, too? This is when opening your hands to a fresh start and a new way of living may help.

Women I work with often add more into their lives without taking things out to create balance, and that often leads to exhaustion. **More and less** is about saying yes to what you do want and no to what you don't; saying yes to yourself to say no to others. It's about walking away from one idea or habit and walking toward something different. Whatever you want more of, chances are you will need to let go of something else that is sapping your time and energy. When you think about what you want, such as more self-love, confidence, or inspiration, you will inevitably need less self-hatred, insecurity, and comparison with others.

As you learn to let go of the things that make you feel less (yes, I know this isn't easy!), I can almost guarantee you that life gets even better. Of course, you can't always see that change clearly while you are in the middle of it. For example, I wasn't thrilled when I got fired from my waitressing job at a fast-food franchise, but a few months later, I got an even better job at a casual dining restaurant that helped pay my way through university and where I met many amazing people.

Job loss can give you time to look for the work you are super passionate about. A breakup can lead to an even better, healthier relationship. A friend bailing on plans may give you the chance to dine solo. Do you have an "even better" example of your own?

More and less is an ongoing swap of one idea, habit, or choice to make room for another and an invitation for you to try other things. There is no one way or one right way; there is only your way. Make it your own and see what happens!

More and Less in Motion

Have you ever thought about what you need more of and less of? Asking yourself "what if?" and then putting your unique ideas into action becomes more and less in action. Designed by you, lived by you!

Let's say you want more time to do things that you love—you will need to have less time wasters in your day. Swap out scrolling social media for a dance class. If you want more money, you will likely need to save more and spend less, regardless of how much you are making. To be healthier, you can choose to eat more whole and nutritious foods cooked at home and spend less on dining out and delivery. You may need to lose an hour of Netflix to put an hour into your shop on Etsy.

Take the time to think about what your more and less list might look like. Here are some suggestions based on what other young women have shared with me as things that they want more of in their lives:

- Self-kindness
- Optimism
- Mindfulness
- Personal time
- Learning and passion projects
- Making a difference

And they would like less of these:

- Screen time
- Body shaming
- Judging
- FOMO
- Tripping about the future

Life is all about both **more and less**. It's filled with twists and turns, bumps and potholes, exhilarating highs, and epic lows. Putting the **more and less** approach into practice means you need to get comfortable with being uncomfortable and be open to change, because at times things are definitely going to be difficult. You may be cheated on, terminated from a job, or rejected from a school program. You will fall and you will rise. But every time you start fresh on a platform of **more and less**, you will have a new experience, learn a new lesson, or take on a new perspective. You have one life, and whether you can take five minutes, give five percent more, or try five ideas from this book, something is always better than nothing.

Why wait? Let's start now so that you can live your version of a bolder, brighter you!

Letter from Lindsay

May I be completely honest with you? I long for a truly authentic, happy, abundantly joyful life. I want to rise up to this life with fearlessness, fierceness, and an untamed heart. Honestly.

Yet sometimes I feel stuck. I am trapped in my need to please, my push for perfection, my self-doubt and insecurities, my fear of falling and failing, and my feelings—*so many feelings*—mostly of the "not good enough" variety.

Do you ever feel this way? Do you go back and forth wanting to be more, but feeling like less?

Let's agree to start fresh from a place of truth with some important beliefs, including the following: You are valuable and worthy. You are strong and brave. You may feel bruised or even broken at times, but you are also resilient and mighty. You may feel worried and afraid, but you keep going and keep trying anyway. You may feel focused on what others think, but you are going to say "so what!" and show up for yourself, embrace your uniqueness, and step into the truth of your real self. Most of all, you are going to start believing in the potential of your possibilities.

I believe you have what you need inside of you: your feelings and sensations, your intuition and sensitivities, your ideas, your knowingness, your passions, your courage, your sparkle, and your truest self.

You deserve a fresh start, and I will meet you wherever you are. I will show up for you, as you learn to do the same for yourself. I will encourage you to be perfectly imperfect and to make mistakes, as you learn to do the same for yourself. This doesn't mean you are flaky; this means you are open to learning and trying new ways.

You have tremendous potential to be a bolder and brighter version of yourself, not just today but every day, not just sometimes but all the time. Choose to lean into and love your truths without apology or hesitation. Don't miss out on the chance to begin again today and every day thereafter. This is your chance to step into a fresh start.

—Lindsay xo

Chapter 1
More Happiness, Less Waiting

To be honest...

Do you ever feel unhappy, but you just don't know why?

Do you find yourself comparing your happiness to the happiness of others?

Do you wonder what will really make you happy?

Do you try to buy or earn your happiness?

Do you expect to be happy all the time and are disappointed when you are not?

Stop buying happiness.

Stop seeking happiness.

Be happy first.

Something Like Happy. This is the name of a book by Eva Woods that stares down at me from where it sits on my shelf. I find the title equal parts resigned, as in "this is as good as it gets," and provocative, as in "are you happy, really?" Every time I glance its way, I have three thoughts. One: I should probably read this book soon. Two: I don't *want* to read this book. Three: I am "something like" happy, a version of happy, truly happy, aren't I? I'm not always sure... this is an embarrassing revelation, but I have tried to eat, buy, and accomplish my way to happiness. That's right, I actually believed these strategies would work!

Over time I have come to realize five truths about happiness: It comes and goes in unpredictable waves. It doesn't last forever but nor would I want it to. Happiness can come my way both effortlessly and through hard work.

I am happiest when I am creating. One bonus truth: I will not settle for *something like happy*. How about you?

One of my clients, Yukari, told me that she feels less happy when she is scrolling and happier when she is strolling. I found her insight clever, funny, and completely true! When Avery came to see me, she told me that as she raced from class to class, appointment to appointment, and social event to social event, she realized she was busy but not happy. She started to do a little less in her day to find more moments where she could simply pause and be. "Doing nothing is so hard," she said, "and yet I am learning that taking time to notice my happiness as it's happening is something."

I know we all want to be more happy. We all try to be happy—something like happy, kind of happy, sort of happy, happy enough but (big but) wanting to become even more happy—and less sad, lonely, empty, and worried. One recent Instagram post I saw said: DO MORE OF WHAT MAKES U HAPPY. "Okay," I thought, "I will!" Where I get lost, and perhaps where you do, too, is figuring out how.

Tyre, who is one of my more happy-go-lucky clients, often asks me, "But how do I become more happy?" That is one question I can't answer for her, but I do let her know that little by little is one of my favorite life philosophies when it comes to happiness. Little by little, what we do makes a difference in feeling more happy and living more happily.

Imagining the happiest version of yourself is the beginning of making it happen.

What If? Then What?

What if you could be even more happy? ▸ *Then would you let go of all that makes you unhappy and embrace what makes you happy?*

What if you took time to notice happiness? ▸ *Then would you see all the happiness you already have?*

What if you hustled for your happiness, each and every day? ▸ *Then would you feel empowered to create your happy?*

What if you took time to consider what makes you most happy and then worked toward your ideas to be really happy? ▸ *Then would you be your happiest self?*

What if you released your expectations of happiness—especially "happiness now"—released your waiting, and defined happiness on your own terms, in your own way? ▸ *Then would you trust that you know what makes you happy and discover what happiness means to you?*

What Is Happiness?

Happiness is a feeling inside of you—you know, that feeling you get when you receive a compliment on your outfit, a free coffee, or that job you've been striving for. Perhaps there is a reason for your happiness, like an idea for a new dish you want to try or an invitation to go to a restaurant opening. Perhaps there is no reason at all but that you had a good sleep, are loving the sunshine, or have one of those days when everything seems to flow your way.

Happiness, often associated with joy, jubilance, glee, delight, and excitement, is the upside of life's downside. Happiness comes and goes. It doesn't last forever, but no feeling ever does or really should. And so often, at the exact moment we notice it, the spell breaks.

Happiness is what we all strive for in all different ways. We wait for it. We long for it. We wonder why we are not happier. Although many of us have every comfort and convenience, which we take for granted here in Western culture, we all seem to be lacking in happiness. I think this is because we complicate happiness when it can be surprisingly simple.

Happiness can be found in simple pleasures, such as a piece of chocolate, fresh flowers, or a friendly chat with a stranger, or in more complex forms, such as a call from the doctor to tell you that all is well or the trip you thought was canceled is happening after all. It can be found in places, people, passions, and pursuits. Many clients tell me there comes a time when buying and enjoying "stuff" stops meaning as much, and they start working on their inner abundance, such as hope and excitement.

Over the years, my clients have shared with me the simple things that make them happy: family trips, hanging out with friends, good food or coffee, and checking things off their to-do lists. One of my clients, Monique, told me that she is "learning that my happiness always comes down to my mental health and how well I am taking care of myself."

Other clients, like twenty-six-year-old Kelly, share their deeper reasons for being happy. She said, "I am happiest when I choose to surround myself with healthy, supportive, kind, calming, and positive people. I used to tolerate those who would judge or question me, and I never felt happy when I came home. I have learned how important it is to be around those who contribute to your happy, not deplete your happy."

In the end, happiness is what you make it. Start by imagining what happiness could feel and look like for you. Then start cultivating and designing it to fit you.

Note to Self

What makes us happy changes. In my twenties I was a waitress, and I earned enough money to pay for my college tuition, buy a car in cash, and save for a rainy day. I also treated myself—I splurged on jewelry, clothes, shoes, a new duvet, and even art! This made me happy at the time. In my thirties with a full-time "real job," I still bought myself stuff as needed but I began investing in treatments such as massages and therapy. This helped me feel healthy and happy. Now, in my forties, I still treat myself but I can feel happy by giving back to others as well. This could mean giving my time in pro bono consultations or presentations, or money to organizations and foundations that are supporting and empowering young girls and women.

Now, this makes me truly happy. What does happiness mean to you right now?

Happiness Is Not . . .

You probably already know what makes you *feel* most and least happy. But have you considered what you *do* to try to be happy? Do you buy more or spend more time on social media? Do you think you will be happy if you have more followers, likes, degrees, pay raises, cars, houses, vacations, and friends?

Figuring this out took me a while but I know now that my happiness cannot be found in more stuff. Don't get me wrong, things like new clothes, shoes, apps, and books can make me briefly happy, most of the time. But the more I acquired in my life, thinking it would make me happy, the less happy I felt. The more I made my happiness dependent on possessions, projects, and people, the more I set myself up for unhappiness—and even desperation—when the happiness ended or left.

Happiness is not something outside of ourselves or something that arrives on our doorsteps. Happiness is not something that just happens. Instead, it is something we feel on the inside, something that comes out of us when we choose to feel happy about who we are, as we are, where we are. I know that's not easy to do, but I'm going to give you some tips on how to shake things loose.

"If anybody has a bad day, they'll just come to my room because they know I'll bring out the positive in everything, or I'll make them laugh, or I'll be just crazy."

Simone Biles
@simonebiles

Why Does Happiness Matter?

As I was researching happiness for this book, one question kept surfacing: Why are we all so *unhappy*? We live in a culture that tells us that we need to be happy now and all the time. But as we strive for more and better, so often we don't even notice when we *are* happy. Or if we do, we dismiss it or feel we don't deserve it. So, we keep searching and continue to feel unhappy. We know something is missing but what? As I searched for information that would help me grapple with the answer to this question, I landed on an article on Psychology Today that helped me gain some insight.

The article explained that happiness is not the result of bouncing from one positive experience to the next. Rather, it takes both time and discomfort. We must also consider the many factors that contribute to happiness such as "genetic makeup, life circumstances, achievements, marital status, social relationships, even your neighbors—all influence how happy you are."[3]

True, and yet I find happiness is also a function of effort. I call this "hustling for happiness," and it is more in our control than we know. There is an entire field dedicated to researching whether we can cultivate happiness. Called positive psychology, this field of research was founded by US psychologist and author Martin Seligman in 1998. Simply put, positive psychology is the study of human flourishing, which includes actions such as showing your appreciation for your loved ones and developing your personal strengths. Using a gratitude journal can also create many happy benefits, such as an increase in self-esteem, improved relationships, and a greater life outlook.[4] Essentially, when we focus on the positive parts of our lives—whether that's events or influences, experiences, or traits such as gratitude and compassion—we may become even happier.

According to Dan Baker and Cameron Stauth, authors of *What Happy People Know*, there are six tools for happiness: appreciation, choice, personal power, leading with your strengths, the power of language and stories, and multidimensional living (relationships, health, and purpose).[5]

People who seem to be putting these tools into practice include Kate Hudson, actress, producer, and entrepreneur, and Michael Strahan, NFL legend turned commentator and TV personality.

Hudson says there is no secret to her happiness. In her words, "when you connect with your breath, and nurture a positive, intuitive relationship with yourself and your body, you will begin to settle and feel in sync with everything around you. This is the essence of health. When we can stay well—adapt to greater stress and have greater endurance—then the joy and inspiration rush in, impelling us forward into life."[6]

In his book, *Wake Up Happy*, Strahan talks about happiness as "an ongoing pursuit, maybe the most important test of our lives. Because at the end of your life, if your stack of happy days is bigger than your stack of miserable days, then yours was a life well lived. It's that simple."[7] I love this idea of a stack of happy days!

Although being happy and living a happy life can sometimes be a challenge, we can't ignore the benefits of a happy lifestyle like improved physical health, a better quality of life, and longevity. This is why your happiness matters!

Whether you are indulging in small pleasures, such as new throw pillows for your bed, a new outfit, or a hot bath, or looking for bigger ones, such as setting academic goals or working hard at a new job, happy people know this: they live with purpose. There is a reason for waking up every morning. There is a point, even on hard days of stress and struggle, and they keep that in mind.

> "I am happiest when I surround myself with healthy, supportive, kind, calming and positive people."
>
> *Kelly Basra Kelemen*
> *@kelkelemen*

5 Ways to Promote Happiness

Write down five of your favorite things in your journal and refer to this list when things seem dark.

Get outside and move your body every single day.

Give yourself (or someone else) a compliment as you think it.

Try a new activity whenever you feel bored or restless.

Connect with others by text, DM, phone call, email, or in person.

What Blocks Happiness?

We want to be happy, but often happiness is hindered in three specific ways: expectations, comparison, and tough stuff.

High Expectations

Iris, a nineteen-year-old college student, once told me, "I expect a lot of people around me, but more so, I expect a lot of myself. I am constantly putting pressure on myself to improve at school, at my job at the grocery store, and with my friends and family."

You may have big ideas about what happiness is supposed to be like and feel like—and you're doing it and feeling it! But some of us fall into thinking traps such as "I'll be happy when I get the job" or "I'd be happy if I was healthier." But when you get "there," you often don't feel how you think you are supposed to feel.

Lots of us get trapped in the expectation-and-disappointment loop. I am also a queen of high expectations. Even though I am making my one life count through these expectations, I'm also setting myself up for disappointments. The problem is expectation can exceed the reality, and you may feel frustrated or disillusioned.

But lowering your standards is not the way to avoid the expectation-and-disappointment loop because standards are excellent ways to develop yourself.

If you find yourself continually anticipating and waiting for life's big happy moments, you might miss out on life's simple happy moments. Instead of waiting for happy, why not try living happily right now?

Comparison

Let me be straight: you will never ever win the comparison game—the game is rigged. There will always be someone who is or seems happier. Many young women I speak with are in a race to keep up with what they see in other people's lives. They may see other women their age online or in their community who are pursuing multiple endeavors, such as creating a small business, traveling, attending school, and keeping a full-time job. But there is no way these women can keep up, so they resign themselves to this thought: "I'll just never be happy."

Don't get me wrong—the images we see online or people we engage with in our everyday lives may inspire us and help us clarify what happiness could mean to us. But most often what you see is not what you get. Seeing other people apparently so happy can be a reminder of how happy we are not. You may adopt a competitive edge by trying to do and achieve more and faster. Sometimes you may even criticize the happiness you see in others as a way to feel better. The very notion of FOMO can make us feel like we are "missing" out on happiness.

So here is something to consider: if you are going to compare, please compare who you are today with who you were yesterday. That's right: compare yourself to yourself, especially when you are navigating tough stuff.

The Tough Stuff

Ready for some truth talk? Life is difficult. Life is challenging. Life is unfair. There will be struggles and setbacks. You may face and endure difficulties such as discrimination, racism, and other inequalities. You may experience the deep disappointment of not getting into a program or school or the job that you wanted. You may lose friends or go through challenging breakups, get ill, or need to support a sick family member. You may endure financial hardship or need to move away from all that is familiar for work. The world is confusing and chaotic, but that is life. However, the "hard" parts of life remind you that you are doing life, not avoiding it.

If you know that tough stuff will happen—not just to you—and you can accept this, then you will be in a stronger position to prepare for it. Life's difficulties build your inner strength and resilience, and when you work through this tough stuff, you will feel happier and likely appreciate your happiness more.

Create your happiness, in your own way!

What Builds Your Happiness?

There is no one way to create your unique happy life, but here are some ideas that you can try.

You Define Your Happy

Happiness is never one size fits all. What makes you happy is going to be different from what makes me happy. What makes you happy today may look different tomorrow. Happiness changes shape and form, every day and in every way. Our pursuit of happiness changes as life changes and as we change also. This is exciting!

Less comparing or worrying about what happiness should be is very likely to generate more happiness. When we let go of the ideal, whether we are talking happiness or something else, and when we stop looking, scrolling, and worrying if we are doing it right, we get closer to what happiness means to us. Check in with your own happiness metrics. Measure your happiness with how you are feeling. It's that easy. We complicate happiness when we search outside of our internal system, our knowingness (see chapter 3). When you decide in your way and in your own time what happiness means to you—not anyone else—you become the driver of your own bus, not the passenger. You—yes, you—can create your sense of happiness, which is unlike anyone else's.

For instance, having busy weekdays and even busier weekends, performing with musicians, and eating out a lot used to make me happy, but these things no longer do. Today, I'm happy when I create fresh posts for my Instagram account or design a new handout (or write my next chapter). I'm also happy being more domestic these days (I can't believe I'm saying that!). I'm learning to cook and even getting into home decor. And I've embraced this truth: I don't enjoy doing too many things at one time or in one day. This is my new happy or my happy now. By contrast, my client Michelen is busy all the time. She is a fast thinker, talker, and mover! I don't think she could fit more in her day if she tried. She loves creating jam-packed days of flow. Feeling productive is her happy place. I can't argue with her—if this works for her, then she needs to go for it!

What makes you happy today? What makes you happiest? Who makes up a happy day for you? What is your happy place? What are happy memories you treasure? What are happy thoughts you can hold on to? Can you think of happy ideas to look forward to? Can you plan to be even more happy? As you consider these questions, you will start to make meaning of your happiness.

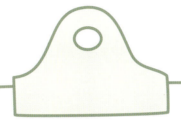

Your Happiness Helper

To help you with your quest for more happiness, try creating a happiness chart. Draw up three columns and label each one with one of the following questions. Fill in each column with as many ideas as you can.

* Happiness then—what made me happy in the past?
* Happiness now—what makes me happy in the present?
* Happiness soon—what might make me happy in the future?

Choose Joy

Hanging on my bedroom wall is a framed print of the words *choose joy*. It's the first thing I see every day and a reminder that happiness comes and goes, but joy—joy is my choice. You choose how you want to see things and what to focus on. At the same time, you can choose not to make excuses for why you are not happier.

From time to time, clients do blame their parents, teachers, bosses, and boyfriends or girlfriends for why they aren't happier. What I share with them is this perspective: sometimes people are responsible for disappointing us, but you can still choose how to respond to that disappointment. You can choose joy—for example, joy that you learned something despite what you feel you are not getting.

I'm not saying don't be sad or down or lean into a bad day. Feel all your feelings. I am saying don't waste time drowning in your sorrows. Start turning your bad day into a good one. Even though you may feel awful, use this as a chance to feel better. Choose your response to what happens in your day. Do something, do anything, do everything you can think of that brings you joy, and I swear, happiness follows.

- Choose joy even when it's hard.
- Choose joy even when you don't want to.
- Choose joy when there doesn't seem to be any available.

"I am letting go of those expectations, and that's opening me up to moments of transcendent bliss."

Anne Hathaway
@annehathaway

Cultivating Joy

Here's a tool I use often, which will help you create joy. There are three ways you can try to cultivate joy: noticing happiness, creating happiness, and planning for happiness.

Noticing Happiness

Pay attention to and be grateful for simple things. Write down five things to be grateful for each day but be specific. Instead of writing "I am thankful for my health," try writing "I am thankful that I had a brisk walk with my dog, and I smelled the freshness of spring." Include appreciation for simple things, such as clean water, your healthy body, your bedroom sanctuary, or a close relationship with a friend or family member. Once you start listing, you won't be able to stop. When you choose the joy in the simple things you have, it boosts your happiness quotient.

Creating Happiness

You can figure out what makes you happy and do more of *that*, but if you don't know, choose one of the following ideas today:

- Talk to a happy person
- Recall a happy memory
- Visit a place that makes you happy
- Look at happy pictures
- Sing happy songs

Planning for Happiness

This is a smart strategy, and believe me, it works. For example, one day I was feeling down so I decided to create a happiness plan: I'd run a new route, try out a new café, meet up with a friend, and start taking photos! For you, it could be having a movie night, a date day with your boyfriend or girlfriend, or catching up on that book you've been wanting to read. Whatever—you guessed it—makes you happy!

Finding the Silver Lining in Unhappy Times

Hands down, my most miserable life moment by far, so far from happy and from home, was when I was in Greece on holiday. I was only twenty at the time and not worldly by any means, so this trip felt really difficult. I don't know if you've been to Greece, but with its breathtaking panoramic views of jagged mountains, the deep blue of the sea, and the tiny white houses adorned with bright red bougainvillea, you'd think you'd be nothing but happy. Nope—not me. I was unhappy with my travel companion, myself, and my current life circumstances. I felt far from home and, worse, far from myself, and all I wanted was to get on the first plane home. I kept thinking "What am I doing here?" and "How do I get back?" I didn't know what to do, but I did know I was unhappy.

Sometimes when you spend some time digging into unhappiness, you do learn more about your happiness. When you hang out in unhappiness just for a while, knowing it's a temporary state of being, that unhappiness can teach you about the silver linings it may conceal.

In the case of my misadventure and homesickness, I can't tell you how happy and thankful I felt to come home and not live out of a smelly backpack. Unhappiness was the reminder I needed of how much I loved being at home and with the people who I felt closest to. It also taught me this gem: geography doesn't determine contentment. Being in a "happy place" and expecting to feel nothing but pure bliss didn't mean I would be happy (remember that expectation-and-disappointment loop I talked about?). I recall feeling betrayed and blue at the time, but I also learned that happiness is inside of me, not in Greece.

Being unhappy is uncomfortable. You want to quickly wiggle your way out and find your normal again. But I encourage you to stay with your unhappiness for a while and trust that something good (or even better) will come from it.

Silver Linings Playbook

It's okay to just be unhappy for a while. Lean in and learn from your unhappiness—there is a silver lining.

Unhappy Experience	Possible Silver Lining
✱ Feeling self-critical	✱ You decide to up your self-care game
✱ Your friend ghosts you (ending a relationship with you without explanation)	✱ You decide it's time to expand and diversify your social circle
✱ You get let go from your current job	✱ You finally have time to create your own business

Self-Interview

What would make you even happier?

When you aren't feeling happy, what can you do?

Can you think of a happy memory and recreate this experience in some way?

If you could pick one thing that could make you "happy now," what would you choose?

Who is the happiest person you know and why?

I knew early on in my teaching career that something was missing for me. I took a chance and connected with a life coach who ended our first meeting with a question that launched me into my least favorite place to be—discomfort. She asked, "What do you really, really, really want?" Instantly, out of sheer discomfort, and also defiance, I responded, "I don't know."

But I lied. I knew exactly what I wanted. I wanted to do the unfathomable: leave my job after just one year. I wanted to create the not-yet imaginable: my own company. I wanted to do the unlikely: follow my heart and find my dreams. Do you know how long it took me to answer that life coach's question? Fifteen years! But I knew. I knew with every ounce of my being. I just didn't believe that I deserved more than something like happy.

Just the other day, my client Zara told me, "I have never been happier." When I queried as to why and what her secret was, she told me, "I think so much of my early twenties was about trying to make everyone happy. Then I read a quotation by Alicia Keys where she told Adam Levine, 'I do what the @#*& I want.' And something inside of me clicked, like, yes, of course, this is my life. I should do exactly what I want and exactly what makes *me* happy!" Eureka!

You know happiness is not instant or constant, but I do believe you can cultivate happiness. You, too, can be more (so much more) than something like happy.

MADE FOR MORE

To be honest . . .

What could even more happiness mean to you?

The More and Less of Happiness

More...

- Playfulness
- Creativity
- Time in nature
- Love
- Connection
- Appreciation
- Laughter
- Joy
- Adventure

Less...

- Sadness
- Worry
- Stress and anxiety
- Fear
- Pain
- Waiting
- Wanting
- Seriousness
- Greed

Chapter 2
More Confidence, Less Doubt

To be honest...

In what areas of your life do you feel the most confident?

In what areas of your life do you feel the least confident?

What are the skills you have that help you to be confident?

What skills do you want to cultivate to boost your confidence?

Who is the most confident person you know and what makes them confident?

> **Focus on what confidence means to you.**
>
> **Credit yourself for doing three things well today.**
>
> **Imagine your confident self— what are they doing?**

Sometimes in my work coaching girls and young women, I have the privilege of working with them from the time they are in their early teens until their early twenties. This was the case with Misha. At first, Misha was quiet and soft-spoken when she did speak, and she rarely offered her opinions. She was also hardworking. Over the years, she started to think more for herself and began to speak up and share her stories, ideas, and opinion. Misha graduated from high school and attended college. She moved out of the city and was living on her own for the first time.

We met for coffee after she had just graduated with her degree in health sciences and moved back home. As I waited at the café with my tall coffee and muffin, in walked a tall, radiant, and very confident young woman. It was Misha, and I couldn't have been prouder of the strikingly self-assured person she had become. What impressed me more were her stories of college and how she had found a great group of friends, figured out who she was without her parents and the safety of home life, and cultivated a love for fashion and photography. If ever there was a turnaround story when it came to gaining confidence, it was Misha's.

I don't know where you are on the confidence spectrum, but I do know that we can always use a little more confidence! Still, every day I meet young women who are having a confidence crisis. Sadly, this crisis tends to start early in their lives.

Around the age of eight, amid a perfect storm of changes, including changing bodies, changing social circles, and most detrimental, a growing awareness of what other girls think of them, some girls start holding back, hesitating, and comparing themselves to others. They are constantly evaluating who is smarter, prettier, more popular, and more talented than they are.

Today, these constant comparisons are magnified with the "help" of apps like Instagram, Snapchat, and TikTok. In a recent *Time* magazine article, Amanda Macmillan stated that "Instagram is the worst social media network for mental health and wellbeing, according to a recent survey of almost 1,500 teens and young adults. While the photo-based platform got points for self-expression and self-identity, it was also associated with high levels of anxiety, depression, bullying and FOMO, or the 'fear of missing out.'"[8]

I wonder if this is why, when asked a question, some girls look to others and wonder what they *should* say while discounting and dismissing what they *want* to say. They fear disappointing *anyone*, so they become determined to please *everyone*. And that's the moment young people let go of their self-confidence to reach for the elusive stamp of approval. Some girls carry this reaction and their lack of confidence into the teen years and beyond. Others are able to shake it off and grow into themselves, with more confidence than ever, just like Misha—and that's what I hope for all young women.

CONFIDENCE

What If? Then What?

What if **you saw confidence as a skill that you practiced every day?** ▸ *Then would you commit to becoming even more confident?*

What if **you were less afraid of what people thought about your confident self?** ▸ *Then would you stop caring what others thought about you?*

What if **you were known as the "confident one"?** ▸ *Then would you feel like a positive example for others?*

What if **you used your voice and owned your space?** ▸ *Then would you see your power and influence as you stand up for yourself and others?*

What if **you doubted yourself less?** ▸ *Then could you be braver and live a bigger, even better life?*

Feel confident to be confident and be confident to feel confident!

What Is Confidence?

Mila shared this nugget of insight during an intense session where we talked about how the past can hinder your confidence in your future. She told me, "It's really a mental game. You have to work so hard to check your thoughts and take care of your mental health. You can only be confident and believe in your value if you are reminding yourself every day you are worth feeling this way. Every day, I tell myself, I am smart, beautiful, and I can accomplish anything."

Mila's words struck me because when I was her age I was lacking in confidence. I started building my self-confidence by doing things like ordering at a restaurant or asking questions even when I was uncertain and afraid that I'd look stupid. Slowly I stopped comparing my inside life to the outside lives I saw elsewhere. What I had to learn is something that Mila seemed to understand already, and that confidence takes practice and time (you'll see)!

Confidence, as defined in an article by Psychology Today, is "a belief in oneself, the conviction that one has the ability to meet life's challenges and to succeed—and the willingness to act accordingly. Being confident requires a realistic sense of one's capabilities and feeling secure in that knowledge."[9]

When you can feel strong and healthy—in your body and in your mind—you own your space and your voice, and you are more able to speak up for yourself and others. With confidence you can take chances and know that you can try new things without doubt. With confidence you are certain that whatever the outcome of your actions, you are going to learn something of value.

Confidence is the belief in yourself—your values, talents, skills, qualities, and aspirations. Confidence is being bold, brave, and when necessary, a little bit badass—fearless, not reckless. Confidence is working through the discomfort of uncertainty—instead of avoiding it—so you can do hard and even scary things. Like happiness, confidence may at times feel fleeting or even lost on some days. Don't worry; you can always get it back!

Confidence Is Not . . .

Confidence doesn't mean that you can be arrogant, rude, or condescending to other people. When you are confident, you don't need to use your voice to dominate a conversation just to be heard. You don't need to boast about your accomplishments or gloat when you win an argument. Needing to feel better than others makes you conceited, not confident.

Confidence is not humility or a humblebrag.

Confidence is not retreating to the shadows because you don't want others to see what lights you up. When you are confident, you don't fear what others think, and you don't pretend that you aren't flawed.

When you are feeling less than confident, remind yourself what confidence is not, and you'll find that true confidence naturally rises to the surface.

"Give yourself more credit than criticism and more grace than judgment."

Kristina Kuzmic
@kristinakuzmic

Why Does Confidence Matter?

A lack of confidence is sometimes equated with a lack of growth. But even though I work with some extremely talented women, they still lack confidence, despite their successes. This emotional reaction is often referred to as imposter syndrome: an internal experience of believing that you are not as competent as others perceive you to be. Some people feel undeserving of any accomplishment and as though, at any moment, they will be "found out" as not being as good as people think.

When my client Desaray earned a job tutoring a young girl, she remembers texting her friends this message: "I'm going to start tutoring a girl in high school pre-calc, and I feel like I'm experiencing imposter syndrome." Later she told me, "I knew I was capable. I knew the material. I had the grades to prove I knew my stuff, but I still felt as though I knew nothing and wondered how I was going to teach this when I wasn't qualified. I let myself believe I was bad at math."

So many of my clients echo Des's experience. They tell me they feel that they don't deserve to be in their classes or programs, they wonder if there was a mistake in the hiring process for their jobs, or they worry that everyone else is smarter and more talented.

I don't think there is any such thing as being too confident. The world needs women like you to be more confident, not less! Even still, young women tell me they feel increasingly sensitive to being "too confident" and they are immensely fearful of being called conceited. So, what do some women do? They downplay their confidence.

But when you don't step into your confidence, you may shy away from conflict or feel upset when misunderstood. Without confidence, you may miss out on the chance to share your ideas and opinions or the opportunities that come your way to be even more confident. Down the insecurity spiral you will fall, feeling unraveled, panicked, and insecure.

Confidence gives you the strength to feel more powerful in yourself. You'll be able to ask for what you need, such as a favor or more time to think, and go for what you really want, such as that all-important first career step, a trip, or starting your own small business. With confidence, you care less about what people believe about you because you believe in you—and this matters even more. With confidence, there's simply no room for doubt and uncertainty inside you, and you have more energy to keep you moving forward. The confidence you feel empowers you to block the noise that seeks to bring you down, to stand strong and secure in who you are and what you stand for.

But what if the notion of either being confident or not confident is too black and white? Instead, think of your confidence on a sliding scale and acknowledge with kindness and compassion that sometimes you will feel more and less confident, depending on what's going on in your life. You are a work in progress!

> "I don't think anyone who has ever spoken out, or stood up or had a brave moment, has regretted it."
>
> *Megan Rapinoe*
> @mrapinoe

5 Ways to Promote Confidence

Develop different skills.

Be an eternal learner.

Speak up for yourself.

Speak out for someone else or a cause.

Take more risks.

What Blocks Confidence?

Many young women I talk with are confused about how confident they are supposed to be. I can see their point because the so-called rules can be confusing and also completely biased and unfair when it comes to how confident men can be (hint: very!). I hear three distinct reasons from young women about what blocks their confidence. Do any of them resonate with you?

Society's Mixed Messages

Seems to me like the day girls are born, a text is sent encouraging them to reach for the stars, be everything they dare dream, break those glass ceilings, and be confident. Right after that, another text is sent telling them to play it safe, do what they can without making others feel insecure, and be confident but not conceited. Confusing? One hundred percent. Although you are navigating rapidly changing times and a resurgence of the women's movement, how powerful you can be is still a mixed message. I say we don't need to be confused or mixed up about this. Instead, we need to be clearly confident. Period.

Jealousy and Judgment

As we grow, even if we do have confidence, being confident among your peers is sometimes tough. Some people are quick to become jealous of confident people and may respond with judgment or criticism. Insecurities in others may get triggered and some find it easier to judge or condemn a confident person rather than ask for their confidence tricks. I love what Rachel Hollis says about insecurity: "Our own insecurities on any subject either spark our curiosity or they feed our judgment. We either see the opportunity to grow and so allow ourselves to wonder, ask questions, and do research, or we become fearful and close down the idea immediately."[10]

At this time in your life, you'll have more opportunity to choose the people in your circle. There will be individuals who celebrate your successes and others who skip over them. Choose carefully! Spend time with people who are sure of themselves so that you can learn from them and lean into sharing your successes.

> **Note to Self**
>
> Truth be told, I can be competitive and jealous. There have been instances when I have grown envious when friends have found "the one" or were promoted or even got more followers on social media. Now when I feel jealous, I try to hold back judgment and recognize that I must want what that other person has, too. If this is the case, I have gained the gift of clarity and so I ask questions and allow myself to feel inspired and excited to get busy.

Self-Doubt

When you hide away from confidence in an effort to maintain relationships or are afraid of shining, this can fuel self-doubt and insecurity. You might tell yourself, "I am not university material" or "I'm underqualified to apply for the job I want." You may find yourself flooded with questions, such as "Do I matter?", "Am I loved?", "Can I really speak up?", and "Do I have what it takes?"

Many young women I work with suffer from self-doubt, especially as this time of life requires them to try many new things. But I also see how many of them are ambitious, and there are times when they are *overqualified* for opportunities that come their way. If you are a self-doubter, hold on to this piece of advice from author, podcaster, and small business owner Ruth Soukup: "The only way to truly overcome insecurities and fears of not being capable is to start proving to yourself that you actually are capable."[11]

Cultivate confidence by building up your competence.

What Builds Your Confidence?

If you are like me, you have always believed that confidence is something you were either born with or you weren't. That is simply not true. Confidence is something that you can work on. Here are three ways you can start to boost your confidence: practice, skill development, and cultivating bravery.

Practice, Practice, Practice

If you want to increase your confidence, hang on to this gem: practice, practice, practice confidence with your mindset, your words, and your actions.

In Your Thoughts

Start with your mindset. Too often, we focus on what we can't do or worry that we aren't capable enough and that there's no room or time to grow our confidence. Instead, begin the day with a confident thought, such as "I can do this" or "of course I can," so you start the day right on positive thoughts—one strong and confident thought at a time.

Thoughts, big and small, influence how we feel and how we behave. In other words, when you choose a strong and encouraging message, such as "I can solve my own problems," the resulting feelings can be pleased, proud, or powerful. And then it happens—you act more confidently.

Here's an experiment that I guarantee is worth your effort. Instead of focusing on the confidence you lack, choose to focus on the belief that you *are* a confident person. As you do this again and again (remember this is all about practice!), you can shape your feelings more positively and confidently. If you happen to notice doubt creeping in, don't worry: you can choose again (and again).

Morning until night—this is how much of each day you will need to think confident thoughts. If you meet each day with certainty, then you will be able to handle what comes your way. Believe that even when you face a problem or something you don't understand, you will figure it out or find someone who can help you figure it out.

When you prevent thoughts of uncertainty and self-doubt entering your brain, you can direct your energy to thoughts of certainty and self-belief. Researchers say it this way: where focus goes energy flows.[12]

In Your Words

Next you need to practice showing your confidence in your words. You know words have power, right? They have the potential to lift up or knock down as well as the power to showcase your confidence. That's why you must choose your words carefully and think before you speak. What you sound like and how you say it reveals to people what you stand for and even whether they should listen to you, believe you, and ultimately respect you.

Have you ever made a mistake and instantly berated yourself—"How could you be so stupid?"—using harsh words and a tone that you would never use with a friend? Confidence starts with how you speak to yourself. Please be kind. For one week, I dare you—no, I beg you—to not pick yourself apart. Use affirmations such as these: I am stronger than my problems; I focus on what I can do instead of what I can't; and I am not defined by my mistakes.

Pay attention to the self-narrative you are scripting and how you speak to others. Many young women are shocked when I repeat back to them what they are saying about themselves. Are you telling yourself "I'll never be happy," "I can't do work and go to school at the same time," "I will always struggle with my body confidence," "I'm not cut out for leadership positions," or "I don't 'need' anyone"?

Notice any little ways you may be making yourself smaller and insignificant, how you downplay your outstanding ways, or dismiss compliments as "no big deal." Take note of when you speak quietly or with hesitation. None of this sounds confident. All of it needs to stop. Here's what a confident person sounds like: "This is what I know to be true . . ." and "Here's an interesting fact I just read last night . . ." and "Of course I can do it."

In Your Actions

Now we get to the acting confident. Like anything we want to become better and more skilled at, it all comes down to practice. You may practice your art or sport; you may invest time in your academic studies or at a volunteer position in your community. As a result, I'm going to assume you develop skills, and your success likely motivates you to keep going.

Let me ask you this: How is confidence any different? If you truly want to become a more certain and confident person, you need to practice just like any other skill. Can you practice being confident? Can you do it for just one day? Or can this be day one? Here's a tool to help you start practicing being confident in your thoughts, in your words, and in your actions.

Total Confidence Planner

Every day, think of one thing you can work on for each category in the following chart. Here are some examples for you to work with, but get creative coming up with your own!

Your Thoughts
- "I believe in myself."
- "I can work through difficulty."

Your Words
- "I will focus on everything I do right today."
- "I've got this."

Your Actions
- Look in the mirror and tell yourself what you like about you, inside and out.
- Make that call you've put off.
- Ask that question.

Competence = Confidence

The stronger and more diverse your skill set is, the more powerful and sure of yourself you will feel. Guaranteed. Unlike the kind of confidence that you may feel when someone compliments or praises you, competence is solely dependent on you and your efforts.

You know what else? Your skill set, which also begins with a positive mindset, is infinite. You can commit to eternal development to grow smarter, stronger, and more skilled, and nobody can take your skill set away from you. Once you develop a skill, it's yours to keep and to keep developing. This is one of the most profound game-changing skills I can proffer you to build and boost your self-confidence.

Take a minute to think of the skills you already have. Many young women I work with have mad skills, but they dismiss their skill set by saying, "But that's easy." Yes, I tell them, easy for *you* because you worked at this for a long time. Here's a sample list of some basic skills that you likely have and may discount.

- Making a meal for yourself or other family members
- Doing laundry
- Posting on your social media platforms
- Asking for what you want or need
- Spending money/giving a tip
- Telling a story/giving an example
- Driving a car/calling a taxi
- Shopping for groceries
- Learning another language

Once you have identified your skills (please, be honest and gentle), think about skills you want to develop. Here are some possibilities that I've divided up into three categories: soft skills, hard skills, and life skills.

Soft Skills

These are skills that express your mindset and ability to manage your emotions.

- Showing empathy
- Active listening
- Asking questions
- Understanding your own emotions and reactions
- Flexibility
- Creative thinking
- Decision-making
- Negotiating

Hard Skills

These are skills that you'd use at school or a job.

- Reading and staying up to date with current affairs
- Writing
- Presenting a talk
- Tech skills
- Researching
- Providing customer service and guidance

Life Skills

These are skills you need for adulting.

- Basic etiquette and personal hygiene
- House cleaning
- Money management
- Organizing and planning and using a calendar/agenda
- Doing oil changes on your car
- Making a major purchase (furniture, a car, a house)
- Self-management of feelings, thoughts, and stressors

Now, from these three categories, choose one skill and ask yourself some questions:

- Why do I want to learn this skill?
- What is holding me back from developing this skill?
- What do I need to get started?
- What is my first step?
- How can I learn about this skill?
- Who can I follow or consult as an example of what this skill looks like when it is developed?
- How much time each day/week/month can I commit to developing this skill?
- What support will I need to learn this skill?
- What will it be like to have fine-tuned this skill?

Cultivating confidence through skill progression takes time and requires patience, perseverance, and practice. When I'm working with young women and they tell me they want to become better readers or more organized, I always talk to them about the fact that their progress is a function of one factor. Do you want to know what that factor is? Effort.

I tell them, "You can work on this skill for one hour each week, and you will grow, albeit slowly. Conversely, you can invest five hours each week and you will grow exponentially faster." What they give is what they can get!

The choice to develop your skills is always yours and, of course, dependent on your priorities. The more you put in, the more you get back, the more you probably want to keep going! Try to see your skills without limits or limitations, whether you want to try archery, go deep-sea diving, learn how to use new software, or become a better listener.

However, if you do stick with a skill and don't feel it's a good fit for you, it is okay to let it go and shift gears. In fact, this is an important part of knowing what works and what doesn't work for you. Sometimes, you need even more determination and grit; other times, you need to let go.

Please remember to choose one skill at a time and to diversify your skill set. You can (and should) be multipassionate, which helps you be balanced and happy.

Confidence Skill Builder

Identify your skill set by using the following tool. Fill in each column with the skills that apply to you.

My Skills	Skills I'm Learning	Skills I Want to Develop
* I can create a website. * I am good with people. * I can choose food that makes me healthy and feel good.	* I am learning to be a better listener. * I am learning how to develop a fitness regime that works for me.	* I want to learn how to edit films. * I want to learn to take better care of our planet.

Be Brave(r)

Zip lining adventures aside, the bravest thing I've ever done is be honest with myself. I'm talking hard-ass truth telling. When I reach "rock bottom points" and think "I have no idea what I'm doing or even who I am," I also get to a real place of "time to get honest, Lindsay." What they say is true: there is only one way to go—*up*. This clarity brings me closer to making changes.

What about you? What's the bravest thing you've ever done? Maybe it's cliff diving or bungee jumping. Obvious risks. Or maybe it's less obvious risk-taking, such as the time you finally told your partner it was over, or when you tried, and failed, to be a firefighter—for the third time. Or when you decided it was time for radical change and you switched degrees or jobs. Bravery is as individual as we are and, in my opinion, worth the inevitable fear and discomfort.

Megan, a client of mine who recently graduated from high school, got her first job this summer. She explained to me that this is the bravest thing she has ever done because it involved so many firsts and she did it all on her own: first online application, first interview, first day of training, and first day of working at a trendy clothing store in the mall.

Bravery is not putting yourself or others in harm's way or throwing caution and common sense to the wind. Bravery is doing what is new and scary, what you haven't tried before, and when you are uncertain of the outcome. Bravery isn't easy or we wouldn't have a bravery deficit. What we need is a bravery surplus. Can you imagine what would happen if more young women went for big opportunities that they felt ready for or created what they believed the world needs more of—art, music, medicine, or ethical businesses? I get excited and hopeful just thinking about it. Now I want to give you two ways to become even more brave: taking risks and asking.

Take Those Risks

Not once have I regretted a risk that I had chosen to take. Regardless of outcome, I always learned *something*—either what I wanted more of or what I wanted less of. But to be clear, I am not talking about risks that are *way* out of your comfort zone. If intuition tells you a person or plan is unsafe, listen to that. I am talking about ideas that feel new, unfamiliar, or have uncertain outcomes but will help you grow.

If you imagine yourself standing in a circle—let's call this your comfort zone—it can feel petrifying to even think about stepping out. This is your safe space, and of course, it makes sense you'd want to stay there—with a duvet and pillow no less. But what if you did take a step and allowed yourself to be uncomfortable? What if feeling uncomfortable was temporary, and after some time, you understood that you are stretching the margins of your comfort zone? Eventually you will feel comfortable, not because you returned to your original safe zone but because your safe zone has widened. This is now your new normal.

Here are some examples of risks that young women have shared with me that stretched their comfort zone:

- Making a mistake/failing
- Changing jobs
- Telling someone how they are truly feeling
- Auditioning
- Joining a new club/group
- Asking someone out
- Saying "I love you"
- Standing up for yourself
- Advocating for social issues

Don't Forget to Ask

Risk-taking is good at getting you out of your comfort zone, but sometimes even learning how to ask for something can be risky. I learned the art of asking when we went on a family vacation to Hawaii. The hotel was under construction when we arrived, but this was not mentioned at the time of booking. I asked for, then earned, our money back. All of it!

I had tasted the elixir, so at this point, there was no turning back. I have asked for deals and refunds, accommodations and help, compromise and time extensions, and compassion and care from others when I am having a bad day. I have also asked for drinks and food to be remade at restaurants, for more clarity when I get my car serviced, and for more anesthetic when the dentist is drilling my teeth. I always ask for answers to my questions and additional information for better understanding.

Asking is the only way to get what you want. But asking may present you with a tricky conundrum as well. It takes confidence to ask (politely), but when you do, and even when you don't know what the reaction will be, you will often boost your confidence in the process of doing so. So what if the answer is no! Maybe next time it won't be.

> "Embrace all your faults. Accept who you are today."
>
> *Mila Rodrigura*
> *@milavanessa*

The Bravery Jar

Take a glass jar and cut up colorful pieces of paper. On each piece of paper, write down an idea for how you can be braver. This could be taking a risk or asking or some other option. Fill the jar with all your ideas (no matter how silly or outlandish). Then each week, choose one brave idea and try to incorporate this into each day.

> I will express my feelings.

> I will try something new I've been avoiding.

> I will make a plan for my health and fitness and start today.

For those of you who choose technology over hands-on crafts, try this: Use the reminders app on your phone so once a day you get a notification for how to feel braver. Or set up some of your passwords (since we have so many) with all your different bravery ideas, such as You_got_this22 or Keep_Going_100!).

Self-Interview

How have you worked to develop your confidence?

Name some examples of when you felt the most and the least confident?

When you lose your confidence, how do you get it back?

What advice or ideas can you offer someone who is just beginning to consider what being confident means to them?

In what ways can you live an even more confident life?

Charlotte is one of my more confident clients, but she wasn't always this way. At the age of thirteen, when we first met, she would tell you that she had little to no confidence. Now Charlotte is in her midtwenties and is setting up her own house-cleaning company. She told me that when we first met, everything scared her. "I remember the first time I took the bus and got lost. I panicked," she said. "I know in elementary school I was always so worried about what all the other kids thought of me, and by the time I got to high school, I'd spend so many mornings feeling sick to my stomach when I had to present in class."

Charlotte knew she wanted to grow in her confidence. She said what worked for her were reciting daily affirmations, trying new things that felt scary on purpose, and practicing using her voice—first in her head and then eventually in front of others. Confidence did grow in Charlotte, but yes, it took time.

Maintaining confidence during the perfect storm of these early years of adulthood, now called adulting, can be challenging. But the more you *practice* confidence, even on days where you have to dig deep, the more you start to *feel* confident. When you show other women you are confident, you offer them permission to be confident, too. Confidence matters, more than we think, and more than we know.

MADE FOR MORE

To be honest . . .

What does more confidence mean to you?

The More and Less of Confidence

More...

* Self-belief
* Positive self-talk
* Speaking up and speaking out
* Standing with poise
* Change and challenge
* Championing confidence in yourself and others

Less...

* Doubt and uncertainty
* Negative self-talk
* Playing it safe
* Thinking you can't
* Waiting to be more confident
* Trying to look like someone else
* Judgment and jealousy
* Feeling ashamed of your confidence

Chapter 3
More Authenticity Less Conformity

To be honest . . .

Do you feel you don't know who you are?

Do you find you focus more on being who you think you should be rather than being yourself?

Do you know how to show up as yourself?

Do you wonder who you could be if you weren't afraid to show your true colors?

Do you worry if you are either "too much" or maybe "not enough"?

AUTHENTICITY

Be you. Do you. For you.

Second grade was magic. It's when I started to understand I was smart and important. But it was also because of one teacher: Miss Zabel.

I remember the first day of school in second grade starting with my outfit: I wore a turquoise button-up blouse with frills, paired with brand-new dark-blue jeans. I eagerly awaited my turn to meet Miss Zabel, and when it was finally my turn, she asked this question: "Would you prefer that I call you Lindsay or Lindsay-Anne?"

Now, this may seem like a simple question, but I grew up in a busy, noisy household where I had to fight for space. I considered Miss Zabel's question quietly, then said, "Lindsay-Anne."

She responded, "Welcome, Lindsay-Anne, to our second grade classroom." She made me feel that I had a voice, I mattered, and I could be true to my authentic self through choosing how I wished to be called. Magic.

Authenticity is different from confidence, though you will need to confidently sort and then clarify your real self. Authenticity is deeper: a knowing of your true values and true colors. Your authentic self cannot be reduced to just one part of you because your truest authenticity includes *all* parts of you.

Take Keira, for example. Keira, who is just twenty-one, describes herself as a bubbly, free-spirited person with eclectic tastes in music, films, and tattoos. Her authentic self also includes her culture, sexuality, friends and family, and her community involvement. She says that early on she knew the world was showing her who to be and that it just didn't fit how she thought about herself. She chose a more expansive definition, and that is how she worked out her own authenticity.

Spoiler alert: If you want to define your authenticity, then you will need to wear your total truth hat. You'll need to ask yourself important questions, such as "How am I doing, really?" and "Am I staying close to my values and beliefs?" Not easy, I know, but completely worth it.

All you have to be is yourself!

What If? Then What?

What if **I told you the most important relationship you can ever have is the one with yourself?** ▸ *Then would you feel you can be yourself, not who the world tells you to be?*

What if **you made time every day to know and love yourself?** ▸ *Then would you practice courageous self-care to feel good about yourself?*

What if **you showed up for yourself every day?** ▸ *Then would you realize that you have value and worth and be more willing to speak your mind with self-confidence?*

What if **you revealed all of yourself to others—your shiny parts and the parts you would prefer to hide?** ▸ *Then would you feel like your whole and honest self?*

What if **you viewed each day as a chance to become even more authentically you?** ▸ *Then would you allow the world to see the authentic you?*

AUTHENTICITY

What Is Authenticity?

Authenticity is your true self: a combination of your values and beliefs, your behavioral traits and talents, your skills and interests, your goals, and your dreams. But authenticity also includes your struggles, stressors, and secrets. Authenticity is deeply knowing your uniqueness. It is not about your *trying* but *being* who you are beyond appearance, accomplishment, and achievement. Authenticity is being able to say: "This is me—real and raw." That knowing allows us to find and create deeper meaning in the *one life* we are given. Before we know, I feel we have to take some time to look at what I call deservability.

I am standing in my closet, deciding on what to wear. For some reason, I start *counting*: twenty-three pairs of jeans, ten sweaters, fifteen fancy summer tops, and a jumble of shoes so messy that I decide to stop counting. I consider how much the contents of my closet are worth—I can assure you this is based on sheer quantity, not quality. Do I deserve all these clothes? Do I really believe that what is inside my closet somehow proves my worth? My closet contemplation leads me to the very concept of deservability.

We are taught that we need to prove our worth, whether that's through achievements, material goods, or big acts of kindness and compassion. But what if we just lived as worthy humans? You are worth it. You may not believe me yet. You will. You may not feel you matter. You do. Repeat after me: "I am worthy. I am worthy. I am worthy." You deserve to feel good, to be happy and healthy, to have love and dreams, to dare to imagine, and to live out loud.

To help you get started, try working with these daily affirmations:

- I deserve to be happy, so I will . . .
- I deserve to be healthy, so I will . . .
- I deserve to make my dreams come true, so I will . . .

You deserve it all, not despite your flaws and mistakes, but *because* of them. You deserve everything you desire in all your humanness and all that makes you, *you*.

Authenticity Is Not...

Authenticity is the opposite of pretense. It is not projecting an ideal image or pretending to be someone else. Authenticity is not changing who you are depending on whom you are talking to and what you are talking about. It is not about giving in to the pressures of this world, and it is definitely not giving up on yourself. Living authentically is not about conforming to what others want to see in you.

Authentic living is not easy, but it does matter. I know how hard it is to be yourself in every situation. Nineteen-year-old Sadie, who left the city she grew up in to attend college in Ottawa to study engineering in French, described to me what being authentic means to her: "I want to show up as me whether I am at work or school, with my family, or meeting new people. It's never easy, but it definitely feels better and it's more work to pretend to be someone you are not."

> "My identity is a superpower—not an obstacle."
>
> **America Ferrera**
> *@americaferrera*

Why Does Authenticity Matter?

Authenticity allows you to embrace both when you flourish and when you fail. Unfortunately, many of us refuse to reveal our authentic selves so that we can feel safe. Yet, when you show your vulnerabilities, this offers others permission to do the same, and that builds connection (see chapter 6). I don't know about you, but when someone shares with me that they are struggling with how they feel about their body, or how they are stressed by their exhausting to-do list, I feel more willing to say "me too." Author and self-professed speaker and cheerleader for her fellow humans, Kristina Kuzmic says this: "Faking it feels miserable and exhausting, and authenticity, though it sometimes feels vulnerable, is freeing and powerful."[13]

Note to Self

There will be times when you cannot (and should not) be your authentic self because it's neither safe nor smart. I have shared a few secrets that were then turned into salacious gossip. I have poured my heart out and received no response from the listener. Practice discernment when deciding who gets your authenticity—when to open up and how much. Guaranteed, you will miscalculate a few times, but experience will teach you how to calculate quickly and even more efficiently when it's wise.

5 Ways to Explore Authenticity

What are five words that describe me today ...

What I know to be true about myself ...

I am most real when I ...

I can be fake when I ...

What I really want you to know about me ...

AUTHENTICITY

What Blocks Authenticity?

On a recent drive to work, I discovered barricades and bright orange pylons blocking my regular route to my workspace, which forced me to take a detour. At first this was frustrating, but eventually I adapted to the new route. Still, it doesn't feel quite right.

Over time, we get used to making detours when we face an obstacle. We shape-shift, we compromise, and often we settle. It's great to be flexible—life demands that—but making detours shouldn't always come at the expense of who we are. Our pleasing and placating selves may earn us the stamp of approval from others, but potentially this costs us the chance to be real. Instead of you—messy, wild, and free—you become that other person who is small, hidden, and acceptable.

I used to be afraid of not being liked or accepted, not being good enough or triggering others' insecurities. That's right—when I sensed someone was uncomfortable, jealous, or even angry with my achievements, I'd simply downplay myself and shift focus to complimenting and lifting them up. Often, I'd explain away my fears with negative self-talk: I am just not good at that (relationship, job, opportunity), or I am never going to be good enough for this (idea, goal, dream). Now, I choose power over powerlessness. I worry less about the opinion of others and more about my own.

In a recent Instagram poll, I asked how many young women in my community felt they were authentic. Only 50 percent said yes. When I asked more specific questions, they told me that they felt authentic in some situations, such as at home and with family and friends, but not in others, such as at work or in new social environments. Many of them, such as Sierra, told me a version of this statement: "I want to be my true self, but I am so afraid that people will judge me and I will be left by myself. I try to figure out who people want me to be—funny, serious, smart—and I have learned to be that person."

Believing in yourself may be last on your list of priorities, but it needs to climb the ladder to the top spot. Instead of giving in to your inner critic, give yourself the cheering and championing you need. Who me, you ask? Of course, you!

Make a choice to show and share a little more of you every day. Just try!

What Builds Your Authenticity?

Picture yourself standing in your underwear and bralette in the middle of Times Square. That's what it may feel like as you start your authenticity journey and get to know yourself. When I begin sessions about self-discovery with young women, some hide behind their hair and short answers, while others zone out by grabbing their phones to escape. I know this work of knowing yourself is hard. But no effort means no self-knowledge. Hard as it may be, once you know, you can't unknow but you will be closer to your most real self.

It took some time, but my client Kingsley began to embrace her authenticity after we worked through the reasons why she felt uncomfortable revealing herself. Here's what she said about that process: "At first, I didn't want to tell Lindsay *anything* about what was really going on for me. As we worked together, I realized what was so difficult for me: I felt that something was *wrong* with me—why else would I be so anxious? Lindsay helped me see that feeling this was normal (and so common), and there were tools we could try to work through my anxiety!"

Many systems and structures in the world lead us away from trusting ourselves: our bodies, our thoughts, our ideas, our creativity. We learn not to trust our bodies when we try to look like the "perfect" bodies we see on social media instead of accepting our bodies' unique shapes and sizes. We doubt and then even hold back our ideas and opinions when we speak up only to receive criticism for what we say, or when we're told to be creative but in a certain kind of way.

It's important that learning how to know yourself is also about questioning your beliefs and recognizing when they are not working for you. This requires time and energy but what you get in return is the truth of who you are. At first you may feel uncomfortable, but this discomfort does not last forever. You will come out on the other side, and at that place, you will know your most authentic self.

Some of what you know about yourself is easy and obvious. You probably already know what kinds of foods and people you like, the types of books you want to read, or the movies you want to watch. Sometimes knowing is instant, like the time I just knew it was time to move out of my family home and live on my own in a new city. Other times, what you know about yourself is far from instant and will require careful deliberation. This can be things like deciding if you want to date online or in person; choosing between buying a used car or leasing a new one; knowing what you want to do after you graduate from college; or figuring out your beliefs about your identity, gender, sexuality, and spirituality, separate from those of your family.

Here's how to get started:

- First, consider your likes and dislikes, your skills and talents, your thoughts and feelings, and what makes you unique, right now.
- Next, go deeper: What do you really need, what do you really want, what matters most to you, and what are you most passionate about?
- Finally, what are your core values? And how do you live by these values?

You may tell people who you are or what you want, but how do you know what is true for you, for sure? Well, sometimes you don't know. Sometimes you'll have absolutely no idea who you are, what to do, where to turn, how to move forward. You'll get it wrong. You'll get it right. You'll have regrets. You'll think "Why did I do this?", "What was I thinking?", or "Why didn't I do this sooner?"

With time and practice, the gap between not knowing who you are authentically and knowing it for certain diminishes. You'll learn to trust yourself because you know how you want to show up in the world for yourself, and for others. Get to know your body, your brain, and your behavior because building your authenticity starts from the inside out and by asking questions.

Know Your Body

Have you ever abused, neglected, ignored, obsessed over, or been incredibly mean to your body?

Our culture, and specifically media images, repeatedly tells young women what ideal beauty should look like from an early age. You've probably seen and heard these messages: there is one shape and size to be; your body is never good enough, so keep trying to change it; follow this diet trend to be fitter and healthier and look your best. Sound familiar? No wonder so many don't feel good in their bodies.

There are people out there countering these messages with the more important lessons, such as listen to your body, trust your body, and know it explicitly. But the proliferation of social media makes it hard to ignore the bad, even though you are following the good messages. Know this: your body is a valuable resource of knowledge, and part of exploring your authentic self is understanding and working *with* your body as it is, how it is.

In my practice, I am fortunate to talk with a wide range of young adults, many of whom identify as women and come with different backgrounds and life experiences. What I've learned is that many of them aren't always thinking about their bodies because they are busy living their lives. However, once some of these young women reach their teens, they start hiding themselves in oversized hoodies or are worried that their bodies are changing in all the wrong ways. They think, "Why can't I just look like that person?"

Unfortunately, for some of these young women, this fixation on how the body looks does travel into the late teens and early twenties. Some are already well practiced at not only condemning their bodies but also fixating on changing them, even to the point of considering cosmetic surgery. They are convinced their bodies are the problem and equally convinced that changing their bodies is the solution. So, they whiten their teeth, straighten and color their hair, tweeze and fill in their eyebrows, add lashes and fake nails, get a spray tan, and inject costly potions into their faces (okay, yes, I have done and still do some of these things, too). It's not necessarily that these changes are wrong, but the constant fixation on them can be damaging (again that expectation-and-disappointment loop comes into play).

But I am also equally aware that other young women love their bodies and don't wish to change a thing. My client Giannina told me that she stays body confident by "learning to embrace myself through appreciating my flaws and understanding that everyone is beautiful in their own way. I don't compare myself to others and I feel comfortable in my own skin."

Honestly, though, Giannina is the exception as I meet so few girls who are this body confident. Perhaps that's due to the nature of my profession, but clients also tell me how prevalent a lack of body confidence is among their friends. For example, I was a little shocked when Devon told me that most of her friends were saving money from their part-time jobs for cosmetic treatment of some kind, such as lip fillers, fat-dissolving injections, Botox, nose jobs, or a BBL (Brazilian butt lift). They were set on changing their bodies instead of changing their thoughts around who they are authentically.

One book I recently read that may have an impact on you is Amanda Laird's *Heavy Flow*. Laird changed my view of the menstrual cycle from thinking it is an annoyance to thinking it is a vital way to monitor my body's health and happiness. One thing that is especially helpful to know is when your ovulating window is—this can be either a life saver or a life creator! Laird says that "your menstrual cycle can tell you about your health and wellness just like your blood pressure, heart rate, or pulse can. Hormonal imbalances, nutrient deficiencies, immunological issues, allergies, and other health issues can be expressed in the menstrual cycle, but you have to pay attention to your cycle in order to see and understand them."[14]

Make yourself a priority, and nourish and nurture your heart and body. This will help you make peace with your body. Another way to do this is to explore moving *beyond* the body. The less you focus on your body, the more time and energy you have to focus on helping, giving, and making a difference. Yes, the body matters, but there is so much more to your life.

One a Day

Every day, without exception, just like you may take a multivitamin, you can choose one thing to do for yourself. Here are some examples but you don't have to do more than one a day!

Choose one of the following activities to nourish your body:
- Eat one fruit, one vegetable, and one healthy fat.
- Try a new food and/or make a home-cooked meal.
- Treat yourself to one guilty pleasure.
- Make time for physical activity, such as a walk outside, a visit to the gym, or a yoga class.
- Embrace a moment of mindfulness (see page 135).

Choose one of the following to move beyond your body:
- Make a gratitude list.
- Perform a random act of kindness.
- Listen to a podcast, read a book, or catch up on current events.
- Work on developing a new skill or on a creative project.
- Reach out to a friend for a call, a meetup, or a video chat.

Know Your Brain

Have you ever found yourself walking or maybe even skipping down the sidewalk, going about living your life, and then you fall into a trap? Not a real trap, though, like on a cartoon. I'm talking about a thinking trap. Perhaps the trap sounds like this: "I got a bad grade on my final paper. Now I won't get into grad school, and I'll never get a job in marine biology." That's an example of all-or-nothing thinking. Or maybe the trap sounds more like this: "I always mess up friendships. I can't seem to get it right." That's overgeneralizing.

Recognizing when I may fall into a thinking trap or getting myself out of one helps me know my brain. I often fall into two common thinking traps. The first I call A to Z thinking: (A) someone will cancel a plan with me and (Z) I jump to a conclusion, such as they hate me. The second trap I fall into is what I call a brain explosion. A simple idea, such as going to yoga class, explodes into a complex array of possibilities, such as taking yoga teacher training and developing my own online yoga courses, and all of a sudden, I'm overwhelmed and not thinking about what I'm doing right now—I'm caught in a future fantasy.

Psychologists tell us there are seven of these thinking traps, ranging from fortune-telling (believing you can predict the future) to mind-reading (believing you know what others are thinking without any real evidence).[15] Whatever thinking trap you tend to default to, it can be a challenge to be aware that you have fallen headlong into one—or to know how to get yourself out.

That's when science comes into the mix. Neuroscience has always intrigued me (even though I'm not particularly "sciency"), specifically the idea of neuroplasticity. In an article called "Want to Rewire Your Brain for Meaningful Life Changes? Do These Things Immediately," Thomas Oppong explains what this concept is: "Neuroplasticity refers [to] your brain's ability to reorganize itself, both physically and functionally, throughout your life due to your environment, behavior, thinking, and emotions."[16] So, simply put, neuroplasticity is the brain's ability to change with new experiences and repetition, to literally choose different thoughts to create new and often healthier thinking patterns.

Rewiring your brain or course-correcting takes focus, attention, and effort, but it is possible. Let me explain how the abstract concept of rewiring your neuronal networks can work for you. Let's say you don't get that amazing job you applied for, you didn't pass an exam, or you forgot to pay a bill on time. Initially you might think, "I suck at adulting." Instead try this approach: be curious about why you are drawing this conclusion and criticizing yourself so harshly. Catch your negative thoughts and replace them with positive thoughts that are more reflective of the circumstances. How about this: "I am learning to adult one day at a time." Do you want to put the icing on the cake? Give yourself a pat on the back or a star sticker. However you reward or acknowledge your efforts, it's critical that you give yourself credit for redirecting your thinking. Over time you'll find that repeated awareness and redirecting your automatic thoughts (new neural pathways) will lead to healthier and more positive thoughts.

Here's the thing: your subconscious mind cannot distinguish between truth and fiction, so every thought you choose becomes your reality. Choose kind, loving, and healthy thoughts that build you up, and you will create a world of kindness, love, and healthfulness for yourself. Negative thoughts promote stress while lowering your self-esteem. Why would you want this? Your thoughts have tremendous ability, so please create the world you want with your positive thought choices!

"If you're feeling low, I am sending you the biggest hug and please know that you are worthy of help and support and you are loved."

Tori Wesszer
@fraicheliving

Brain Power Questions

This exercise is designed to help you become more aware about how and what you are thinking, especially when you find yourself being self-critical.

Check In
- What am I thinking?
- Why?
- What prompted this thought?

Challenge
- Is this thought true?
- Can I think of evidence for and against this thought?
- What else could be true?

Change
- Can I create a more balanced and positive thought?
- Can I reframe in a new way?
- Can I consider a different perspective?

Just like your body, your brain needs your attention. The brain is complicated and also simple because it needs a couple of things to feel good: safety and stimulation. How do you provide this? Take care of your brain with adequate sleep, water, and nutrition, as well as good stress management. Make sure you add stimulation in the form of experiences, such as learning new things, trying different activities, and exploring other ideas outside your worldview.

Know Your Behavior

Raise your hand if you have ever said yes to an invitation or an opportunity, but you really wanted to say no. Or perhaps you have experienced the opposite: you said no to doing a favor for or going on a date with someone, but you really wanted to say yes. Sometimes, to complicate things even more, you might say yes and *then* say no!

Do you wonder things like "Why do I keep buying things I do not need, I already have, or I cannot afford?" or "Why do I scroll through social media when I am not looking for anything?" When it comes to your behavior, these WTF moments can leave you scratching your head in confusion. Well, this section is all about moving from confusion to clarity when it comes to how you act.

Why do we choose to go against what doesn't work for us, like drinking coffee at night when we know it disrupts our sleep or doing a favor for someone when we have absolutely no time? Or why do we want to change yet don't?

Many young women I speak with feel pressure to please or not cause disappointment. Some are concerned that, if they really do what they want, they will cause discomfort in their family or circle of friends. Zsófia told me that where she's from originally, there is a lot of pressure to go to school and earn multiple degrees. Her family is full of doctors, and she does love medicine, but not school. She constantly feels that she's letting her family down by choosing to work for a year and then consider what's next for her rather than racing into medical school. It's never enjoyable to deal with someone else's difficulty with your choices. Yet, how you behave must be true for you and should be aligned with your beliefs, values, and what you really want.

Being authentic and living your values emerge when you consider your "whys," such as:

- Why am I so negative toward myself?
- Why is this person my friend?
- Why don't I take more time for myself?

Take a moment to think about what your answers would be to these "why" questions.

When it comes to everyday lifestyle changes that help us know what we want more of and less of, you probably already know what a challenge it is to change. Why is changing behavior so difficult? Mostly because when behaviors are familiar, they are comforting, even if they are neither helpful nor healthy. That means you need to take an active approach to dislodge them. How we act is the result of years, even decades, of habits and patterns that can take as long to change. You are likely to do what you've always done, but once you know another way, don't you want to do better? It's hard, I know, and yet, in the words of Glennon Doyle, author of *Untamed*, "We can do hard things."

When you become more aware of your own actions (or inactions), you can decide if you want to change. Know this: you do not have to. You can stay the same. But if you do want to change, I'd like to suggest creating some gentle guidelines for yourself. These guidelines, designed by you, reflect your authentic self and are flexible to change with you as you change (your mind, your expectations), but they still offer you the structure and guidance you need to shape your behavior.

> "I intentionally make changes, not because I am lost, but because I have found that my authentic self is change!"
>
> *Kayla Graham*
> *@Kayla.graham_*

Creating Authentic Guidelines

Here are some questions to ask yourself when creating your own guidelines:

* How much water do I want to drink each day?
* What types of food do I want to eat?
* How much sleep do I need to feel rested and rejuvenated?
* How do I want to move my body?
* How much time do I want to spend on social media?
* Is there a new habit that I want to start today?
* Who are the people I know that feel like the right fit for me?
* What are my top five goals or dreams, and what is one action I can take today toward one goal/dream?
* What will I do when I make a mistake or a wrong turn?
* When I notice I'm behaving in a way that doesn't match my values, I will ....
....
....

Self-Interview

> What makes you authentically you?

> How have realizing and knowing your authenticity changed your outlook?

> Can you name examples of when you feel the most and the least authentic?

> What advice or ideas can you offer someone who is just beginning to consider what being authentic means to them?

> In what ways can you become even more authentic?

AUTHENTICITY

I hadn't seen a former client named Karolyn for some time when I ran into her at the clothing store she works at. She had struggled to figure out who she was and her place in life, so I was curious what she was up to now. Karolyn was beaming with pride as she explained that, yes, she had gone through several seasons of feeling lost. She went to college but was not enjoying it until she discovered how much she loved archaeology. After an incredible and eye-opening trip to Peru, Karolyn was now applying to attend a field school of archaeological research. Turns out, her authentic self liked to work with her hands and discover relics. I was so proud of her for both discoveries! I told Karolyn how delighted I was to see how she had grown and embraced who she is authentically.

Authenticity is one of those qualities that many young women circle back to and rediscover after a time of questioning. Thinking about who you were as a young girl can often be illuminating. For example, remember Miss Zabel, my second grade teacher? This past summer I called Miss Zabel to ask her one important question: "What was I like as a little girl?" She told me, "You were so sweet, very smart, and always wanting to help others." I was astounded. Why? Because this is still my essence, my authentic self. Yes, I have grown in many weird and wonderful ways, but my truest, most authentic self was always inside me and is still there today. I need not fear it, feel shame, or hide. It's time to shine, and I need you to shine, too, as we head to our next chapter on progression and hard work!

To be honest . . .

What could even more authenticity mean to you?

AUTHENTICITY

The More and Less of Authenticity

More...

- Self-awareness and being present
- Being your true and whole self
- Vulnerability
- Making mistakes
- Permission to change and grow
- Experimenting with different versions of you
- Exploring the unfiltered version of you
- Accepting the challenge of being real in a fake world

Less...

- Hiding
- Taking yourself too seriously
- Filtering and fabricating
- Detaching from yourself
- Hiding your feelings
- Holding back your opinions and ideas
- Hesitating to be you
- Pleasing others
- Self-doubt
- Being a victim
- Getting stuck in your own story

Chapter 4
More Progress, Less Perfection

To be honest . . .

Do you ever feel overwhelmed by choice?

Do you become frustrated that you are not moving fast enough?

Do you have difficulties making and sticking to a plan?

Do you feel pressure to become your best or to be perfect?

Do you procrastinate for fear of failing and falling?

Do you want to move forward with dreams but don't know how?

> **Every day . . .**
>
> **I will make one choice to move me forward.**
>
> **I will focus on one thing I want to accomplish.**
>
> **I will notice my effort and growth.**

Repeat after me: Progress is not perfection. Progress is not perfectionism.

Perfectionism can make us feel stuck and unsure of where to begin or even if we should begin, but progress is the opposite. Progress is all about moving toward growth. Nobody ever said that progress needs to be big or instant. Usually, progress is slow. No need to keep trying to fast-forward your life. Understand that progress takes time *and* comes with setbacks, failures, wins and successes, hard days, times when you wonder if you should give up or give in, and moments when you can look back, see how far you have come, and be proud of yourself. Progress is not about any destination; progress is the journey to be enjoyed.

I have to tell you this about progress: my whole life I had always earned the "most improved" awards. Most improved player, member, and leader. Embarrassed, I wanted to hide from the glaring spotlight that highlighted the fact that, well, I sucked! Yet, one day, my super talented, highly accomplished colleague Molly confided something that articulated exactly how I have always felt. She said that it doesn't matter what it is, she always struggles at first in her pursuits.

Suddenly, I was able to see my "most improved" awards in a different light: I was recognized because I was diligent and persevered. That's what counted. Taylor Swift articulates this beautifully in her song "Mirrorball," in which she says she has never been a natural and all she does is try. Progress is a necessary step in your life. It's the sign that you are moving forward. It just may not always feel that way.

When I asked several clients about their strategies for progress, many admitted that they are frustrated about how they try and try and try yet still feel that they are getting nowhere. Sometimes they said they got lost in the journey. For example, my client Hannah wanted to set up her own jewelry-making business. She had a passion for handmade jewelry and couldn't wait to share her creative flair with clients. There was one problem: although she wanted to work on her company full-time, she still had bills to pay. So, she waited tables at a restaurant by day and then crafted jewelry and updated her website at night. Hannah is a perfectionist, so getting her jewelry "just right" was paramount for her. She was working but unable to see her progress. This is when the support of her friends came in handy, reminding her where she began—with an idea—and where she is now: in the process of creating her own company. Hannah could see her growth, and this was the motivation she needed to keep going!

Progress is better than perfect.

What If? Then What?

What if you tried to be just a little better than yesterday?
  ▸ *Then would you feel you are growing and changing?*

What if you let go of the idea of perfect? ▸ *Then would you feel you had permission to try to simply be your best?*

What if you understood how procrastination is usually based on fear? ▸ *Then would you let go of avoiding challenging tasks and start doing tough stuff?*

What if you set intentions and took just one step toward a goal each day? ▸ *Then would you feel ready to achieve what you really want?*

What if I told you the only way forward is daily commitment and self-accountability? ▸ *Then would you see progress is your choice and only you can decide to get moving?*

What Is Progress?

Progress is growing a little every day over time. Progress is you—in flow and in flux—evolving without critical self-evaluation, looking forward, not backward. It is rising to challenges without fixating on limits. Progress requires reflecting and reviewing ways to improve as you keep going. It's about reaching for more and better and rising to the best version of you. Progress is seeking out and embracing options and opportunities. I truly believe that personal growth is work and progress moves you closer to fulfillment and purpose.

Progress Is Not . . .

Progress is not the pursuit of perfect, which can hinder your progress altogether. When you want to be perfect, procrastination may be the result. You decide not to try because you don't want to make messy mistakes. Progress is not about avoiding nor is it about hiding from the work you know you need to do.

Progress is not about extremes or obsessions, big leaps. Neither is the journey of progress devoid of mistakes and missteps. Progress is not missing out on the meaningful, messy parts of life but rather meeting yourself in the middle of your mess. It's not staying stuck or stagnant, but rather finding the fire inside you so that you can forge ahead and become that girl on fire!

Why Does Progress Matter?

Nikaiya, who is in her midtwenties, is just completing her postsecondary program in massage therapy. She told me, "I think that what excites me about growth is that there are so many parts of yourself you can unlock when you advocate for yourself. I guess I mean advocating outwardly, but I also mean advocating inwardly against the parts of you that you are hiding or that are hindering you from moving forward. I have grown the most in taking accountability for my feelings, speaking up, and working through my hurt and obstacles."

For a minute, just picture your life without growth: no changing, no improving your skill set, and no development. You wouldn't get stronger, smarter, healthier, or more mature. You'd feel frustrated, stuck, and miserable with nowhere to go and nothing to do. You'd literally be floating through life without direction, plans, or purpose. With no clear goals on your mind or in your agenda, you may feel you are lost and floundering. You may also feel you are wasting your time and even your life. Remember your one precious life!

Progress is an everyday practice. Take it from Jordan Lee Dooley, author of *Own Your Everyday*, who says this: "I'm the definition of a girl who is learning as she goes, figuring out how to trust God has a plan, all while having wacky unfigured-out dreams in my head."[17] And that's the key—we don't have to have anything all figured out. We do have to try. The pursuit of progress is what allows us to grow into being bolder, brighter, and better. And to do that, we need some goals!

In a PositivePsychology.com article titled "The Importance, Benefits, and Value of Goal Setting," Leslie Riopel asserts, "Setting goals helps trigger new behaviors, helps guide your focus and helps you sustain that momentum in life. Goals also help align your focus and promote a sense of self-mastery."[18]

Young women tell me all the time how they have specific goals and can't seem to get going or keep going, especially when they are putting in effort and not getting anywhere. I get it. I do. It can feel frustrating to not be instantly fruitful, but there is purpose to the pain—you are getting ready, and something is happening, even if you don't see it right away. Despite bad days and feeling defeated or deflated, or long stretches of time when you may feel you are working in vain because you don't see any evidence of progress, please know that *something* is still happening—you are growing—and that is progress. The two go hand in hand.

It took me a long time to build my business—and I'm still working on it every day in any way I can. Progress is a forever kind of thing, as long as you stay dedicated to putting in the time. Whether you are achieving, succeeding, and kicking some life butt, or struggling, waiting, or coming up short in the game of life, it's all growth for the good of your development. Progress should be your nonnegotiable.

"What defines you is what you do after your mistakes and how you learn what is meant to be learned from those moments."

Jennifer Lopez
@jlo

5 Ways to Promote Progress

Notice your own growth.

Ask for help.

Compare yourself only to yourself.

Keep developing your skills.

Celebrate along the way.

What Can Block Progress?

Your progress can be easily blocked by what I call the toxic trio of perfectionism and procrastination, making mistakes, and your mean girl inner critic.

The Perfectionism and Procrastination Cycle

Perfectionism and procrastination are two different sides of the same coin, and both can block your progress. Both express black-and-white thinking (remember this thinking trap?)—it's either all or nothing. I'll be perfect or I won't even try—I'd rather avoid doing it than fail or not do it well.

And then there is the perfectionism loop. It goes like this: you have an unrealistic idea of perfect. You feel there is such a thing IRL, so you strive to be perfect, whether that's in your looks, in your relationships, at school or at work, or on social media. When you fail to achieve anything less than perfect, instead of thinking that something is wrong with the concept of perfect, you conclude there's something wrong with *you*. So, you push yourself to the point of being overworked, overwhelmed, and overtaxed!

I could tell you to "let go of perfect" and you might look at me like I'm asking for your last breath. Actually, I appreciate that as a perfectionist you are likely to be hardworking, conscientious, detail oriented, and responsible. Instead, let's change how we view perfectionism. There is no such thing as perfect, but there is such a thing as progress. You can still strive for your goals and big dreams. However, it's important that along the way, you focus on the small steps of achievement, notice your own growth, and become aware of your movement forward without comparing yourself to others.

The Magic of Mistakes

Making mistakes proves two things: you are trying and you are taking chances. Mistakes are the magic! You will make mistakes. So what? What matters more is the "now what?" When you make a mistake, it's what you do after the mistake that counts more. With each mistake, notice and take responsibility for your error. Forgive yourself and give yourself grace and compassion. Then decide to learn, change, and grow. Mistakes are meaning-making experiences. So basically, I'm saying this: make more mistakes, not less.

The SOS Solution to Your Mean Girl Inner Critic

Your critical self-talk is holding you back. Fortunately, there's something you can do. Master your mean girl with this SOS trick. Here's how this goes:

- **S**ee your mean girl every time she pushes herself into your head. You have to acknowledge her so that you can deal with her.
- **O**ppose her. Remember that what she says is so far from your truth. When she offers you a lie, counter her with the truth. If she says you are not good enough, know this means you are more than enough.
- **S**tand up to her and for yourself. Have some phrases prepared to speak back to her with confidence and conviction. Try "I may make mistakes, and this is how I learn" or "I am so excited to keep growing and developing my skills and talents as I aim to accomplish great things."

Step by step, this is how we grow.

You are a work in progression, not a work in perfection!

Progress is your dedication to this mantra: "A little better every day."

What Builds Your Progress?

Ava is one of the most hardworking clients I have ever worked with. She comes to me for coaching, and she spends a lot of time practicing self-coaching. She often arrives at our sessions with timelines, charts, and mind maps. She wants to acknowledge her progress with me. She shows me the beautiful and colorful displays of her growth, and I feel honored to celebrate her progress with her.

What's most interesting about Ava is how far she's come. She will tell you that there was a time when she didn't know where to start on her growth journey, so she didn't do anything. Nada. She felt so stressed and anxious about "all she wanted to accomplish," but she just couldn't start. Then one day it hit her. "I asked myself, 'What is one thing I can do right now?'" she said. As she explains, doing one thing helped her feel more competent. One thing led to the next thing. And many things led to a lot of things, or to put it more articulately, she made progress. Ava lived out what I want to unpack here as positive ways to build your progress: going for your goals, designing your day, and celebrating growth.

Going for Your Goals

When I was in my midtwenties, my family moved from the home I grew up in to a smaller and newer house. As I was packing my most treasured keepsakes, I found this: a pop bottle filled with small pieces of paper. Instantly, I remembered what I had done but forgotten until that moment.

When I was in my late teens, I filled this bottle with the goals I wanted to attain in the next ten years. As I unfolded each piece of paper, this is what I read: graduate from university, buy a car, move into my own apartment, travel to Europe, and become a teacher. I could feel the tears streaming down my face, so proud of my younger self, the self who decided to clarify her goals, and made them happen.

Progress is all about goal setting. Getting started may be the most difficult part of goal setting. You may have so many ideas that you don't know where to start. Or you may have no ideas. But whether your goal is to save for a car, become more tech savvy, or cultivate more happiness in your life, creating goals begins with the fun part—daring to dream.

I know it may feel daunting to try to create a picture of your future, but also know it may feel exhilarating. Take time to playfully imagine what you want your goals to be. You could think "A year from now, I'd like to have . . ." or "Wouldn't it be great if . . ." This is your chance to bring back the "what if" strategy and practice it. I can't emphasize enough how important it is to have an open mind and consider all possibilities. Dream big, then dream even bigger. And remember what to do if your mean girl inner critic tries to sabotage your fun (see page 112)!

After you've settled on your goals, I suggest you choose one to focus on for now. Set the goal, but be specific. So instead of "I want to be more environmentally aware," try this instead: "I will commit to five changes in my lifestyle habits to be a better steward of the planet." Then divide the goal into smaller goals. For example, this could mean that you bike to work instead of drive; you purchase a water filter instead of a case of plastic water bottles; you don't run the water while you brush your teeth; you reduce, reuse, and recycle as much as you can; and you take half an hour each week to learn from experts in environmental issues. See? Clear ideas are more likely to propel you into action.

Now write down your goals because visual reminders encourage you to keep going and keep you on track. Experts say that when goals are written down, those ideas become part of our subconscious and increase the likelihood that we will pursue them. You can create a list, put it on the wall, add entries into your iPhone notes app, create a vision board of images, or add pins to a Pinterest board. Write it down; make it happen!

If writing down your goals doesn't feel like your jam, you can also create mental images—I call these mind movies. I do this all the time, seeing my goals and dreams as a series of scenes, seeing myself giving a big speech to a captivated audience, finishing my book, and starting my media tour. I believe "see it to believe it" is absolutely true.

Once you become familiar with setting a single goal, you can try creating monthly goals. On the first of every month, I have a simple practice. I take my colored markers and draw an imperfect circle (recall "perfectly imperfect"), and I divide the circle into six segments. Then I choose six areas of my life in which I want to grow. I often include work, money, people, creativity, health and fitness, and challenges. Then I list ideas for how I can grow in each area. Since my circle is customized to what matters most to me each month, I can do as much or as little as I want, depending on what's happening for me. Also, next month I can refresh the categories and make changes as I choose.

Whether your goal is learning how to code or strengthening your connections, you will fall and fail at least a few times as you go. Thinking that anyone is good at anything from the start is ridiculous. We are all capable of the "most improved" award. You will feel incompetent and uncomfortable, until you start to improve. The point is this: you've got to trust in the process, and you have to keep going, step by step. Concentrating on one goal at a time and making monthly goals can help you when you get to the next step in your growth and progress.

"Personal growth and development are work, but it's where you get back to your core—who you truly are before rules and expectations."

Susan Elstob
@islapearllife

Time Trackers

As long as I can recall, I've created timelines, which I usually make in January and then tweak in July. There is an exciting duality to these time trackers—seeing what you are accomplishing as your year unfolds and seeing what you set out to accomplish as you keep moving forward.

Here's how to set up your timeline. Grab your colored markers and blank paper (or poster board or use software). Draw a horizontal line from the left side of the page to the right. Space out the months of a year, decide on categories (each to be written in a different color), draw lines either up or down from the timeline, and plan when you want to reach each goal. The timeline gives you a reality check of where you are at and where you hope to get to. You can also use the timeline to reflect and celebrate goals achieved.

JAN	FEB	MAR	APR	MAY	JUNE	JULY	AUG	SEPT	OCT	NOV	DEC
	Find a new apartment		Clear my debt		Research counseling programs				Start online dating		Go on a vacation

Design Your Day (and Your Dreams)

I want you to live your day by design, not default. In other words, I want you to be intentional, not accidental. The reason I say this is because I truly believe that when you learn to manage your day, make and keep a plan, and do what you set out to do, you'll know with all certainty that you can shape your day and your destiny and that it is possible to not only have dreams but also make them happen.

So, let's say you have set yearly goals and you are practicing monthly goal setting, too. Now, you need to try day-to-day goal setting and test your ability to self-manage. How you prepare and plan out your day really does begin with mastering your morning.

When I speak with clients about their daily habits and routines, they confess things like "I wake up at eleven" or "I roll out of bed and head straight to class." As I dig a little deeper, I often learn that they stay up quite late, usually with devices in their hands. They are not alone on this one! So, I think it's fair to say mornings begin with evenings. Here are some quick tips for an evening wind-down plan:

- Consider reducing eating, drinking caffeine, and using screens at least an hour before bed.
- Have a bath or shower.
- Prepare yourself mentally by creating a "wins" list of how you succeeded that day, as well as a list of your worries.

When you get a good night's rest, you can wake up early. Have you heard of the 5 a.m. club? It's real, and it really is a game changer—and when the "let's get going" hormone, cortisol, is at its highest.[19] Not ready for the early rise? No problem. At least aim for a reasonable call time. Then you can choose what your first habits will be. I'll share mine with you here: I wake up at 5 a.m., drink water with lemon, have coffee and journal time, then I run (which often involves planning my day in my mind). When I'm ready, I create a to-do list—all I want to accomplish for that day. I try not to look too far into the next day. Many of my clients have slightly different mornings. They may meditate, walk their dog, or catch up on daily news headlines over breakfast. It doesn't matter what you choose as your morning habits; it matters *that* you choose.

Note to Self

We all have the same twenty-four hours in a day. Picture three coffee cups, each representing eight hours. One coffee cup is for eight hours of sleep, one is for eight hours of work, and the third coffee cup is for whatever you choose to fill it with: time with your pets, writing in your journal, sketching, taking a bubble bath, listening to an audiobook, or tidying up your room or apartment! When you see the visuals, it helps and even inspires you to think about what your third cup of coffee could include and what activities you want to "sip" every day!

Again, how your day unfolds is decided and planned out by you. You can do more, if you choose, and also less. Of course, you need to block out time for activities that you need to do, such as work and school, and what you are responsible for, such as getting enough sleep and preparing food.

But your twenty-four hours also has room for what you want to do. I've learned that life gets boring when we only do what is required of us, so I use my weekly planning sessions to also list what I want to do, such as self-care, things to look forward to, and rewards. This makes my week balanced and something to look forward to. I make appointments with the doctor, dentist, and chiropractor—and with myself, calling them "me time" appointments. If I have blocked off my schedule for my time to get my nails done or get creative, I guard that space like a Labrador protecting a newborn baby!

Remind yourself that "there will be days like this," as in some days you will be slow and sluggish, and other days you will be fast and flying. Some days will be tough and a real challenge; other days will be easy breezy. If any one day feels like too much, you can always shift a to-do to another day of your week.

As much as I love the security and predictability of weekly routines, I have learned to appreciate the freedom and flexibility that comes with the weekends. Weekends are a chance to make some changes, such as sleeping in, taking longer to eat, spending more uninterrupted time with people, and of course, catching up on Netflix. I take time on Sunday nights to get ready and to consider both all I have to do and all I *want* to do. I write out the days of the week—Monday to Sunday—and what I need to get done. If a day looks too full or not full enough, I make changes. This might look different for you, depending on your school or work schedule, so adjust as needed.

When it comes to goals and progress, you might ask, "How do I know I am improving?" To safeguard yourself against deflation and giving up, track your progress. Not with calorie counting or a scale but with the number of times you hit a goal each day.

I give myself a check mark each time I hit a daily goal. Want to know my current list? Subject to change without notice: healthy habits I want more of—such as meditation, water, greens, and reading time—and unhealthy habits I want less of—such as gum chewing, swearing, and screen time.

There is no penalty for not achieving my goals that day and absolutely no pressure, but this list serves as a reminder to try again tomorrow. This way, I am measuring and monitoring, and I can see my effort and progress even if I don't see tangible or instant results!

> "As long as you take every opportunity to learn more about yourself and fall more in love with yourself every day, you're doing good."
>
> **Zendaya Coleman**
> @zendaya

Triple Time Motivators

This is another method for noticing your own growth. When you don't know how to get started (or when you don't *want* to get started), try these three tricks: the fast fifteen, the half-hour hustle, and the power hour.

Decide what you want to focus on with 100 percent attention and intensity. Set a timer for either fifteen, thirty, or sixty minutes and go. This activity does not require finishing. Instead, consider: "How much can I get done in this time frame?" The game aspect may appeal to those who like pressure or competition and also those (like me) who need the time structure—as in, eventually there is an end.

Try the fast fifteen for:
- Catching up on news headlines
- Tidying up your room or apartment
- Stretching or meditating

Use the half-hour hustle for:
- Laundry or dishes
- Catching up on emails or bills
- Cleaning your car

Try the power hour for:
- Exercising
- Reading
- Preparing for a meeting/conversation/project

Celebrating Growth

So many young women that I work with don't notice or celebrate all they do—whether it's getting out of bed in a season of low energy or depression or getting a new job. Some fear that celebration looks like boasting, and some hold the belief that if they celebrate themselves, they will somehow jinx additional accomplishments.

Others are simply full-on when it comes to celebration! My client Jordanna has a close friend, Haroop, who loves to celebrate everything from birthdays and anniversaries to the end of the work week and even the summer and winter solstices! She feels "you only live once" and "life is worth really living!"

I'm an awful celebrator. Correction: I used to be an awful celebrator. Case in point, I graduated university and ran a marathon without a party. Celebrating, though, is as important as setting and achieving goals. You need to take time to look back and notice how you've kicked some butt because this can motivate you to keep going, keep growing.

Please know that celebrating looks different for everyone. Another way of saying this is make your celebrating unique to you. Think about times you have celebrated—either yourself or someone else. What did that look like? Now think of other ways to celebrate. Here are a few ideas I gathered through conversations with young women:

- "I like to post on social media and I love the affirmations I get from followers."
- "When I am proud of myself, I want to share it with my best friend. We have learned to jump into each other's joy."
- "I reward myself with a new adventure—something outdoors that engages my body and gives my brain a break."

Celebrating is a wonderful way to validate your choices and honor your commitment to your goals. It's also a tool for rewriting that script that says "I can't" to "I can," because you just did! It's not about *how* you celebrate; it's about *that* you celebrate—in small ways, in big ways, in all ways. Now, I celebrate all the time. You think I'm joking. I am not. Sometimes, I simply celebrate the fact that I survived Tuesday!

Your Celebration List

Much like a grocery list that helps you stick to what you need—fruits, vegetables, eggs, and toilet paper—and not what is fun to buy—cupcakes, pizza, and magazines—create a celebration list to help you stick to your celebration practice. Remember, you are celebrating small and large steps—all movement is progress! You are even celebrating setbacks and failures. Here's what your list could look like:

Here's What I Am Celebrating . . .	Here's How I Am Celebrating . . .
✱ Going to bed at 10 p.m. and waking up at 7 a.m.	✱ Sipping a latte while listening to my favorite playlist
✱ Sticking to my monthly budget and recording all my expenses for "extras"	✱ Creating a Pinterest board of what I am saving for next
✱ Getting my bike ready for a weekend of mountain biking on new trails	✱ Buying myself a new helmet and water bottle

Self-Interview

In what areas of your life are you progressing?

In what areas of your life are you stuck or trying to be "perfect"?

Knowing that energy creates energy, what is one small step you can take today toward one goal?

What are a few times when you have felt the most invigorated by your progress?

How do you like to celebrate your progress and growth?

I had to smile when Bridgette's mom called me to ask if I could coach her daughter to clean her room. I asked her mom what else she was noticing about Bridgette's behavior so that I had a better handle on how she was doing with everything else in her life. Her mom shared that, although Bridgette was exceptionally intelligent, she was a terrible procrastinator. She didn't hand in assignments on time and was failing or just passing some of her classes as a result.

When I met Bridgette, I was impressed with her mature demeanor and her high energy. She knew that she procrastinated, but she also knew that she worked best under pressure. She liked doing things last minute, and she liked doing things her own way. So, yes, I coached her on time management and organization and helped her keep track of assignments and due dates, and Bridgette did get through high school.

Years later, I received an email from Bridgette's mom, thanking me for my work with her daughter. She told me that Bridgette hadn't gone on to college but decided to start her own business. She found her passion for textiles and developed a clothing line. Get this, she is now a successful entrepreneur (and yes, still has a messy bedroom!).

I know there is a tendency for people to see success in terms of monetary measures, but my takeaway (and her mom's too) was this: Bridgette progressed in her own way, and she found her way.

MADE FOR MORE

To be honest . . .

What could even more progress mean to you?

The More and Less of Progress

More...

* Step-by-step growth
* Patience and perseverance
* Imperfection
* Mistakes and failures
* Daily habits and goals
* Pauses and rest
* Flexibility
* "Good enough"

Less...

* Self-criticism
* Pushing
* Harshness
* Black-and-white thinking
* Comparing and competing
* Stagnation
* Floating and floundering
* Rigidity

Chapter 5
More Mindfulness, Less Distraction

MADE FOR MORE

To be honest . . .

Are you constantly looking at your phone?

Do you ever feel scattered, "spinny," and out of control?

Do you constantly forget appointments, to-dos, items you may need?

Do you have trouble feeling calm?

Do you have a hard time being present and feeling balanced?

MINDFULNESS

Just BE . . .
In a feeling.
In a conversation.
In a moment.

Confession: I am the most distracted person I know. Correction: I *feel* like the most distracted person on the planet. Recently I went grocery shopping and bought everything except the one thing I needed. In the shower I shampooed my hair, but I was convinced it was for the second time. A few weeks ago, I paid for gas and then drove away, at which point I realized I hadn't actually pumped the gas. See: distracted. I swear, I never used to be this way. I used to feel incredibly focused, calm, and grounded. Customers at the restaurant I used to work at would tell me that I had "such a calm energy." My scattered ways are usually for three reasons: I am either thinking, creating, or stressing, all of which are magnified by spending time on social media platforms and, to be honest, screen addiction. I know I am not alone on this one, as some of my clients tell me how hard it is to find peace, especially in a stressed-out, digitally dependent culture.

Katie told me she gets so distracted by noise and groups of people and her own thoughts. She said, "It feels like everything around me is so demanding of my focus, I just lose myself." Lauren told me she often runs up to her room and can't remember what she's looking for when she gets there because something else has distracted her, whether it's her iPhone or laptop or simply her jewelry box on her dresser.

Sometimes my clients *show* me how distracted they are when they are late for appointments, or they miss appointments altogether. They forget to respond to text or email messages and sometimes even struggle to keep up with a conversation.

Granted, not all of you feel or act in this way. However, my sense is that we all want to feel more calm and in control, and certainly less distracted, but we just don't always know how to do that—or do we? The quick answer to that question is that we can create more calm in our lives through mindfulness. I'll talk more about what mindfulness is in this chapter, but simply said, mindfulness is about becoming more aware of your own thoughts and life, other people, and the world around you. Jon Kabat-Zinn, the renowned mindfulness expert, defines it as a way of "connecting with your life."[20]

Believe that mindfulness matters. Just breathe. Just be.

What If? Then What?

What if you were less distracted? ▸ *Then could you focus and pay better attention to each moment?*

What if you made time to tune in to yourself and slow down? ▸ *Then would you make fewer mistakes and have even more time?*

What if you could be more aware of your stress? ▸ *Then could you feel calmer and more in control and learn to cope better?*

What if you learned to face emotional discomfort? ▸ *Then would you be ready to step into more health and wholeness?*

What Is Mindfulness?

According to Jay Shetty, author of *Think Like a Monk*, "Today we all struggle with overthinking, procrastination, and anxiety as a result of indulging the monkey mind."[21] Monkey mind is originally a Buddhist concept that refers to being unsettled, restless, or confused, so much so that your brain is easily distracted. Key to calming your monkey mind is the process of mindfulness.

Mindfulness is attention and attunement to your words, thoughts, and actions. It is an *all-in* experience. All of your focus is directed to what you are sensing, feeling, and doing in the moment. We can be mindful about anything. For example, if I eat mindfully, I slow down, smell the different aromas of my food. As I start to chew, I taste each flavor and sense each texture so that I can truly appreciate what I am eating. If I walk mindfully, I notice the ground below me with each step and what's flowing around me, whether that's the wind blowing through the leaves of the trees or the warmth of the sunshine on my face. I like to think of mindfulness as an active way of living, where you can be your truest self. Mindfulness can be where you feel most awake and alive.

Ultimately, mindfulness is about giving your full attention to whatever it is you are doing at the moment, whether that's breathing in meditation, moving your body, working, or connecting with others to decrease your stress and help you feel more attuned and alive. Of course, most of us aren't 100 percent mindful because the monkey mind is constantly jumping around in the background. But we can become more aware of how our monkey minds are taking over and gently bring ourselves back to the present moment. It's an ongoing process that takes practice because your mind is always active. I like how Dr. Caroline Leaf, a cognitive neuroscientist, describes it: "You can go three weeks without food, three days without water, and three minutes without air, but you cannot go three seconds without thinking."[22] Think about that: three seconds!

Mindfulness has no boundaries. You can be mindful any time you like, for as long as you like. And since your brain wants to feel safe, secure, and calm, mindfulness should be a priority for all of us.

Mindfulness Is Not...

If mindfulness is *all in*, then mindlessness is *all out*—out of step, out of sync, out of sorts, and out of alignment with yourself. This can often cause feelings of being "out of it" or feeling "off," and the result is often distraction and disengagement.

For example, have you ever looked at an empty silver wrapper and thought, "Where did that chocolate bar disappear to?" Or perhaps you've scanned your bank account like a defense lawyer and said, "It's impossible that I spent *that* much money this month." If you answered yes, then you have experienced mindlessness. It is so easy to be mindless. We can mindlessly talk, shop, scroll, eat, shower, or make the bed.

There are so many misconceptions about mindfulness. Mindfulness is not about clearing your mind of thoughts—it's about understanding your mind. Some people view it as a religious or spiritual practice. Others think it is opting out of the tough stuff or detaching yourself from the world because that appears to be easier than coping with all the challenges that life presents. But as an article published on Psychology Today says, "nothing could be further from the truth. It's actually about connecting and embracing life with all of its chaotic beauty; with all of your faults and failings."[23]

> "Meditation really helps create not only a sense of balance ... but serenity and a calm state of mind."
>
> *Eva Mendes*
> @evamendes

Why Does Mindfulness Matter?

Cultivating your mindfulness can positively affect your overall health. In a *Time* spotlight story called "The Art of Being Mindful," Kate Pickert explored the necessity of quieting a busy mind to deal with stress. She says that "rigorous mindfulness training can lower cortisol levels and blood pressure, increase immune response and possibly even affect gene expression. Scientific study is also showing that meditation can have an impact on the structure of the brain itself."[24] In our stressed-out, digitally dependent, multitasking culture, you can see how the ability to be mindful does matter to you and to our world.

But I also see mindfulness as an entry point to something bigger: thoughtfulness. The more mindful you are, the more self-aware you become, the more kind and caring you can be about the larger idea of humanity. Here's an idea: What would happen if every human worked to be more mindful, then more thoughtful? What if we agreed to regularly think beyond ourselves to others? Wouldn't that extend into a more kind, caring, peaceful, and loving humanity?

When I see how some individuals respond to the world's social problems of climate change, poverty, racism, war, and hunger—oblivious, at best; dismissive at worst—I do feel disheartened. Thankfully, there are many other people who don't react this way and are making change, in large and small ways, to combat these issues in any way they can. However, this can also feel like such a big responsibility that you may naturally want to escape. I have the privilege to *not* think about things that feel uncomfortable and some days, it feels like "solving the world's problems" is much too much for me. Do you ever feel this way?

Here's the thing: although the world's problems are not yours alone to solve, your mindfulness practice is something you alone are responsible for. This can show up in different ways. You don't need to sit on a meditation cushion for hours or practice yoga every day to be mindful. Instead, think about how you can be mindful in your day-to-day actions. This can show up in different ways, such as listening to a friend's story without judgment, not buying clothing from the fast fashion industry, and walking or running outdoors without being plugged into your phone. (That last one is a tough one for me, too!)

Mindfulness can infuse your life with more calm and more balance. And it's something you can start fresh with every day, in your own way and in your own time.

"Pause, breathe and listen... being fully where you are is the highest form of mindfulness."

Ayse Camci
@ayse.camci.yoga

5 Ways to Promote Mindfulness

Focus on one task at a time.

Check in with yourself: "What am I sensing right now?"

Take a five-minute break to focus on your breathing.

Try a stretching or yoga class.

Sign up for a mindfulness app like Headspace.

What Can Block Mindfulness?

Before I dive into how to generate mindfulness, I need to talk about what so easily gets in the way of mindfulness: distractions, overwhelm, and being "too busy." Think of these three obstacles as three siblings. They share similarities like siblings share genetics, but they are also different.

Distractions

Distractions can derail you from progress and priorities as one distraction becomes another, then another. Ultimately, they keep you from being anything close to mindful. When I asked several clients and other young women I know to identify their distractors, these were their top five: screens, people, worries, choices, and clutter. How many of these resonate with you? If it's more than two out of the five, it's no wonder you may feel you need to "do it all" but get "nothing done."

I have learned the most about distraction from my clients with ADHD—attention-deficit/hyperactivity disorder—or ADD—attention deficit disorder. Sofia, who was recently diagnosed with ADD, will readily tell you she mostly struggles with getting started and staying on task. When she received her diagnosis, the why of her behaviors finally made sense. She'd always wondered why she'd find half-eaten bowls of cereal or forgotten cups of coffee throughout her house. Now when she is too focused on fine-tuning each PowerPoint slide well into the midnight hours, or not focused enough to read and comprehend information she needs or wants to know, she has learned to practice the perfect pairing. Move over peanut butter and jelly, here comes the perfect pairing: distraction and decision. This is a simple but brilliant strategy that I use often to keep distraction at bay, and you can, too.

Here's how it works: when Sofia notices she has lost focus, such as avoiding an assignment by doing a Google search, she anticipates the rabbit hole she's about to jump into and makes a decision. She sets a timer and allows herself minutes, not hours, to search. When the timer goes off, she returns to her work. Or say she is making a meal. She will turn off her smartphone notifications, so she doesn't message friends instead of cooking her food. If an idea pops into her head while chatting with her boyfriend, she will write a quick note to herself and come back to the idea later. Sofia actively practices the perfect pairing technique to promote focus and mindfulness.

Overwhelm

We all want fluidity and flow to our days instead of stress and upset. But sometimes things don't turn out quite the way you expected. That's when you need to pause and reset.

After a day of running multiple errands, I sometimes return home wired. Fatigued, starving, with a coffee spilling over one hand, I am overwhelmed. For me, overwhelm happens when I appear to be juggling everything well and then something happens, and I come undone. Occasionally, I am overwhelmed by too much to do and not enough time to do it. You may feel overwhelmed from time to time but in different ways. Perhaps you are deciding between too many options, tracking countless passwords, trying to keep up with new technology, or dealing with a lot of school assignments or work deadlines.

But when I do find myself in this place of overwhelm, I stop and make a plan, a step-by-step plan. For example, when I arrive home feeling this way, I stand in my doorway and create a mental checklist that goes something like this: "Lindsay, put everything down, and take off your jacket and shoes. Take everything out of the bags, and put them away. Turn on the kettle, go to the bathroom, and then reward yourself with a fresh cup of coffee." If I take the time to slow down, I can often reset myself and dissolve my overwhelm.

Too Busy?

My grandpa was a hardworking raspberry farmer, so I come by my productivity honestly. "There is always something to be done," he'd tell us. I am not *always* busy, but as a multipassionate entrepreneur, I am responsible for my busyness and doing many things at once; this is, after all, what earns me money. Standing still could mean profit loss. This makes me energized and, sometimes, out of balance.

Often, I even forget what balance means. But what I have figured out is that, instead of striving for balance, I should expect that there will be times when I am more and less busy. My mom once said to me, "When you have too much to do, do nothing." Likely, I laughed, because I thought she literally meant *do nothing*. But then I thought, "Okay, I can see this." Doing nothing can just mean taking time away from the things that are distracting and overwhelming you.

I've learned the value in this "do nothing" strategy by taking quick pauses to check in with myself: "How am I doing?", "How am I feeling?", and "What's next?" I've learned to take pauses in my day—a walk in the park near my house, a text chat with my mom who helps me take a break from rushing and racing. Just a little time gives me the chance to refresh.

If Saturdays are for speeding through some life catch-up, Sundays are for slowing down. I tidy, I putter, and I wander. I do what I feel, when I feel, and as I feel, all to become rested, rejuvenated, and revitalized! Some of my best ideas and solutions emerge after I rest. Whether you take a few minutes or an entire day, play around with this "doing nothing," and find a rhythm and flow that works for you.

Take a pause to reset.

Turn off your device.

Tune into your breath and your body.

What Builds Your Mindfulness?

Mindfulness is all about directing, or redirecting, your attention to where you are and what you are doing at that moment, so you feel less compelled to distract yourself by looking at a screen, making a snack, or even tidying your room. It's all about attention, cultivated through the power of presence, practicing self-calming, and working on healing what may be causing you to feel disengaged and disconnected.

The Power of Presence

Have you ever noticed that as people wait—for the ATM at the bank, in the line at a restaurant—we look for something to do, and most commonly we look down at our phones? To escape a minute of boredom, we check out the weather app, play a quick game, or send a text (guilty as charged).

So many of us seem to be moment-averse, but I think we all crave presence as well. I want to be present when watching a movie, listening to a sermon at church, and getting my hair done. I hate the fact that when something ends, I sometimes feel I have missed the experience.

"I feel like life is passing me by," said Lily in one of our sessions. When I asked her what she meant, she explained that balancing her work as a dental hygienist and her photography side hustle often left her feeling she was always going somewhere, but she was never quite in the moment. Since Lily is a "I am a work in progress" kind of person, she told me she was practicing five minutes of mindful breathing daily and making one intention for the day (no more), such as "today I will be more curious about myself and less critical." These small changes were helping her let go of the "I'm missing out" feeling and feel more attunement in her mind, body, and passions.

Presence is being open and available; being ready to pay full attention to what is happening for you and immerse yourself in an experience. This allows you to notice yourself, others, and situations and respond appropriately. This could mean really *feeling* a hug, tasting your food, or enjoying a good laugh. It's saying, "Hello, today—here I am!" I see presence as the intersection of noticing, feeling, reflecting, evaluating, and adjusting.

What if you shifted to enjoy being present in a moment? Instead of filling every moment with something, try leaving moments empty and spacious—room to be and to feel—like that doing nothing I talked about earlier (see page 142). With presence comes really feeling, really thinking, and really being.

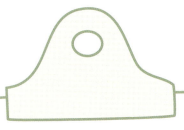

Single Tasking

I love multitasking, and our society glorifies this lifestyle. We even boast to friends that "during a video call, I turned the camera and microphone off so I could eat and check out Craigslist for a new apartment." But dividing your attention like this means you are only half paying attention and half understanding. As an alternative, try single tasking, which asks for your full attention, focus, effort. See if you feel better about what you are doing—and if you get more done with more awareness of what you are doing—when completing the following tasks without reverting to doing something else at the same time.

* Cooking
* Doing your homework (although listening to music too is okay!)
* Going for a walk
* Reading a book
* Watching Netflix (without scrolling on your phone at the same time)

Finding Calm

Imagine this is an Instagram story poll: *Can you find your calm: YES or NO?*

Which one would you tap?

I ask because many young women I talk to are challenged to find calm because they feel constantly stressed and anxious. But before I talk about finding your calm center, let's talk about what's on the periphery of it—stress and anxiety.

When you experience a stressor or trigger, your body will show you that it's in stress mode with signs, such as a change in body temperature, an upset stomach or headache, or a buzzing feeling. Your body will protect itself by launching into fight, flight, or freeze mode. Then you will want to cope and feel better. You might choose some unhealthy (yet completely understandable) coping tools, such as binge-watching Netflix, overeating or sleeping, drugs or alcohol, or gaming. Or you might choose healthier alternatives, such as journaling, exercising, music, or meditation.

An even better way to cope is to notice the stressor and pay careful attention to your interpretation. Let's say someone doesn't text you back, and you tell yourself that this must mean you've offended them. Check in with yourself and the story you just told yourself. This is *one* interpretation, and yes, your brain is a meaning-making machine, but it is not necessarily an accurate interpreter. If you stay in neutral statements, such as "all I know is the person hasn't texted me back yet," you can better manage the stress cycle from its early stages.

Calm may feel like a foreign concept some days. After all, how can you feel calm when you are dealing with financial, relational, or emotional stress or when you are struggling to keep up? In your next stressful moment, you may want to try these ideas:

- **Ask yourself what's in your control:** The weather, people's opinions, or the news cycle are *not* in your control. Your mindset, your schedule, and your life's outlook *are* in your control. Just asking and answering this one simple question may calm you.

- **Unburden yourself:** This is an effective strategy that I suggest to my clients when they know they have a busy mind and want to create more headspace or heart space. Write this in the middle of a piece of paper: "What's on my mind?" and then brainstorm everything that you are thinking about. I use different colors so I can see the separate ideas. When you have released everything on paper, you may find that you've created brain space for yourself.
- **Use the three Ds:** Look at the ideas you wrote on your paper in the previous step and make some choices. I call this the three Ds: **delete** (not necessary or not a priority), **delegate** (ask for help), and **do** (take action).

As you work with these ideas, your perspective may shift and help move you from disorder to order, from uncertain to certain—all contributing to a greater sense of calm.

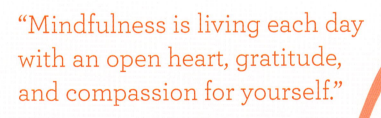

"Mindfulness is living each day with an open heart, gratitude, and compassion for yourself."

Amanda Beisel
@sknclinic

Get Grounded!

Perhaps you already have a few calming techniques you go to regularly. Perhaps you flop onto your bed and hide under your duvet, strum a few chords on your guitar, or reduce your caffeine or sugar intake. But sometimes you need to connect with your five senses to ground yourself. You may want to try some (or all) of these grounding techniques.

* Squeeze Play-Doh (or knead real dough if you love baking) or a stress ball.
* Put on your favorite hoodie, use essential oils in a diffuser, make a cup of tea, and pay attention to what you see, hear, feel, touch, and taste.
* Try some breathing exercises. Here's one to practice called the 4-4-4 method: inhale for 4 seconds, hold for 4 seconds, exhale for 4 seconds.
* Take it to the mat: practice yoga.
* Memorize a poem, sing a song, read some affirmations out loud, or practice another language you are learning.
* Dry brush your body to exfoliate and then alternate having a hot shower with a cool one.
* Take a power walk or a favorite exercise class and enjoy getting sweaty.
* Try a social media break and talk to friends who boost your mood.

Healing Your Hurt to Find Wholeness

Healing from hurt is hard. Finding your way back to wholeness—something that I define as a calmer place where your hurt isn't affecting your daily life constantly—can be a challenge, depending on the depth of hurt you've experienced. I'm not going to talk about hurt and trauma in all their shapes and forms here because they vary so much from person to person. You may not have received the love and attention you needed as a child, or you may be currently struggling with some of life's disappointments and letdowns, or you may have experienced traumatic events that require the help of professionals.

Whatever it is that you are facing, ultimately finding your way back to feeling whole and healed is not a straight line and will require your ongoing attention and mindfulness. Feeling whole again does depend on how much awareness you can bring to your healing, although I understand it may be painful. Yet there are some positive and powerful steps you can take right now to begin that process.

Avoid the Blame Game

When a close friend handed me a truth bomb—"Don't be a victim"—I was defensive and distraught and then I landed on acceptance. Turns out, I was blaming lots of people for my circumstances: my parents for putting too much on me at such a young age, employees for their inability to recognize my contributions, and my friends for not showing up for me. Life hack: Don't blame because nobody ever wins the blame game.

You might be struggling with mental health or tolerating toxicity. You may be experiencing chronic fatigue, racism, sexism. You may be feeling held down, set back, and damaged. You may be complaining about your life and criticizing other people for theirs. You might blame your parents, your teachers, or the system for the lack of care, money, or support in your life. The hard recognition here is that it is easier to blame others for our actions and circumstances and much harder to take responsibility for our own healing.

Bad things happen. But berating yourself or self-punishing doesn't help you heal. It's possible you've been on the receiving end of others' harmful actions or even abuse. I'm not saying you don't have every right to feel like a victim. But, for me, when I took a step out of my own misery, that's when I could see that I was not alone—everyone has stories of heartache, struggle, and pain.

Take Small Steps

What sets apart victims from victors is—you guessed it—their actionable steps that push for healing. Take the time you need; take small steps toward claiming back your wholeness. My healing journey has included lots of talking, buckets of tears, and amazing people who held space for me, listened without judgment, who "got" me.

I've also had the privilege of holding space for many young women who needed healing. It all starts with one small step. Samantha reminded me of this in our work together, and on one tough day for her, I gently told her to let her tears fall and that I would just sit with her until she wanted to talk. She needed me to take that step with her before she could reach a place where she was ready to talk about the next step. Maybe you have a close friend, a parent, or a trusted professional who can be this support for you. Whoever they are, allow yourself to take that step and be helped.

Stand Up and Count Yourself

I have a big ask of you: Can you dig deep, let go of excuses and obstacles and find the resilience to stand up and fight for yourself? In this world you are going to have to advocate for your voice, your happiness and healing, and your right to wholeness.

When I look at women who have done great things, many have had to confront difficulties and challenges. Take athletes like Serena and Venus Williams, politicians such as Kamala Harris and Jacinda

Ardern, education advocate Malala Yousafzai, environmental activist Greta Thunberg, poet laureate Amanda Gorman, equality and women empowerment ambassador Meghan Markle, and journalist Lisa Ling. They could have easily given up and given in, but they didn't. They kept going, kept fighting.

> **Note to Self**
>
> I have trouble forgiving people who have harmed me. Getting to the place of forgiveness felt impossible because it felt like giving in and losing. Yet, I figured out a way to "win" in a different way: forgiving but not forgetting. Yes, forgiving and releasing myself from my rumination allows me to move on, but not forgetting allows me to learn from the experience. Yes, there is compassion and I want to extend this to people, but I want to also be mindful of people's true colors. I am also learning the power of grace, giving people second chances when I see they have changed!

Forgive

Nothing will get in the way of being more mindful than hanging on to pain. So, just as you use soap to wash and clean your hands, forgiveness will clean your heart and relieve you of your burdens. Still, I want to tread carefully on this subject because there is *no* excuse for abuse or neglect. Zero tolerance. I need to also say that if you are a victim of abuse, you can and need to heal. Please seek professional help.

Sometimes we need to forgive people for the hurt they've caused—their cutting words, their mistakes and misconduct—and we can. Sometimes, we need to forgive ourselves for being self-critical when things get tough or self-harming to feel better. There is freedom in forgiveness, in extending grace to ourselves and others. What that looks like is up to you. If you cannot have or don't feel comfortable having the conversation with the person who has hurt you, that's okay. Instead, you can choose to write a letter or email that never gets sent, have an imaginary conversation with an empty chair, or share your story with a trusted friend or counselor. With forgiveness comes a release that may free you of a burden you no longer need to carry and allows you to move forward.

Expand Your Support Circle

Look for the people who you can lean on for help and advice as well as healing and optimal health. My support circle includes a therapist, doctor, accountant, hair stylist, acupuncturist, and car mechanic (because car repairs stress me out). As your needs change, so will your circle. There may be people already in your community who are ready to help. Community can offer you a sense of belonging, a chance to share your stories, and support ongoing growth. Whether you find community in a physical space, such as a church or community center, or a virtual one, such as social media groups or private platforms, community is central to the human experience.

Ponder and Post It

The lovely thing about self-love is that it also builds your mindfulness as you check in with yourself. With each act of self-love, you are reminding yourself that your love for yourself is unconditional; it is not based on your body, job, soul-mate status, activity level, skin quality, or bank account balance. No way. Your self-love is much more: it's falling head over heels in love with all of who you are. Try these ideas for a week and track how you are feeling by the end of it.

* Write out your ideas for self-love, and put them on sticky notes all over the place: on your bathroom mirror, in your wallet, on the refrigerator. This can be a great reminder that your well-being is your priority!
* Put positive messages in your devices: on your desktop, as passwords, or as reminder pop-ups: "You are so lovely," "You are doing your best," "I am so proud of you today."
* Take one hour each day to practice loving yourself: engaging in mindful meditation, reading your favorite book, watching a sunrise or sunset, getting a manicure or pedicure, writing in a journal, or messaging friends.
* Write yourself a permission slip as a reminder that you are human and worthy of love: Today, I grant myself permission to do exactly what I need to love myself. I, _____ [your name], give myself permission to _____ [be playful, quiet, silly, carefree; take a chance, a break, the day off; try worrying less, thinking less, stressing less].

Self-Interview

What does being mindful mean to you?

What have you learned about mindfulness so far?

What are some obstacles when it comes to your being more mindful?

If everyone in the world was a little more mindful and thoughtful, what would the world be like?

How do you find time to be mindful?

As my client Brooklyn started her fourth year of postsecondary school and considered moving out of the family home, she told me, "The world keeps changing, which makes it harder to stay balanced, focused, and mindful. There are so many more options—at the coffee shop, in the cereal aisle, degrees or diplomas, in-person or remote work, and even ways to date. Then there is the blinking, flashing, buzzing, and pinging—so much to look at online, click on, scroll through, and respond to—all demanding and dividing your attention, keeping you from feeling anything but focused, calm, and mindful."

Brooklyn came into one session completely overwhelmed by her to-do list and her day. Together, we strategized a way that, to this day, works for her when she is feeling this way. Since so many choices are out of her control (and can cause choice anxiety), we focused on the choices that were in her control. Her list of things she could control included her mindset, her mood, her daily plan, the time she spent on her screen, and her top three priorities for each day.

More mindfulness is a tool that can help you with all the life stuff that comes with adulthood, all of which can be exhilarating, terrifying, and daunting. But like many of the things I've talked about in this book, mindfulness is not a constant force and needs practice. Basically, your attention needs attending to! But you are in good company because many of us are challenged by this.

I use the same tools I suggest to my clients to find calm and practice mindfulness. It is hard for them. It is hard for me. It is difficult for us all. Yet, deep down, we know what feels best and what we need to do to generate a sense of peace and wholeness.

MADE FOR MORE

To be honest . . .

What could a fresh start on mindfulness mean to you?

MINDFULNESS

The More and Less of Mindfulness

More...

✸ Awareness

✸ Attention

✸ Attunement

✸ Thoughtfulness

✸ Balance

✸ Slowing down

✸ Empathy

✸ Self-love

✸ Healing

Less...

✸ Distractions

✸ Ignoring or denying

✸ Spending and scrolling

✸ Spinning and stressing

✸ Wasting time

✸ Multitasking

✸ Blaming

✸ Rushing

✸ Carelessness

Chapter 6

More Connection, Less Separation

To be honest . . .

Do you have many friends but often feel lonely?

Do you wonder if there is more to relationships than swiping right?

Do you ever feel something is wrong with you when it comes to friendship—maybe you have too few friends, too many, or none?

Do you long for connection but just don't know how to create it?

Do you find you settle for unhealthy relationships because you feel that somebody is better than nobody?

Connection matters. Connection is key.

One of my most intuitive and emotionally attuned clients, Alexa, was having a hard time connecting with her partner, Adam. I asked her what was hard about connecting with him and she said, "I feel so judged. Instead of listening to my feelings, he gives me the solution—*his* solution—and expects me to always do what he says." I asked her to think about connections that are easy for her. This relaxed her, and I could see how these new thoughts brought a smile to her face. "We share our troubles, stories, and feelings. There is usually laughter, inside jokes, knowing glances, and such a beautiful level of comfort that we can say anything and be who we really are to each other."

Relational connection is complex because humans are complex. Everyone comes with their own backpack of past experiences, fears, insecurities, unmet needs, and expectations. Despite the messiness of connection, it seems to be the one thing we keep seeking again and again.

I often boldly declare I do not *do* relationships; I don't want to chat about the weather, gossip over coffee, or spend time with people who accept help without reciprocation. I don't have friends, I state. I don't *want* friends. *Then something happens.* Something always happens that pushes me to reconsider my declaration. I encounter stress, and all I want is connection. No. I *need* connection—a heart-to-heart to tell my story and feel that someone "gets me." I long for connection. Actually, I love connection. What about you?

Connection is a feeling of belonging so you can show up as your whole self.

What If? Then What?

What if you could be more connected and share all of who you are in your relationships? ▸ *Then would you feel you belong?*

What if you let go of an idealized image of friendship and create your own? ▸ *Then would you feel you are doing it your way?*

What if you made people a priority? ▸ *Then would you feel more connected?*

What if you stopped compromising by accepting unhealthy behaviors? ▸ *Then could you cultivate a healthier relationship?*

What if you set and kept boundaries? ▸ *Then could you be clear about what you expected, accepted, and rejected?*

What Is Connection?

Connection is meaningful closeness in a relationship: feeling seen, heard, valued, and validated. It is the invitation to show up as yourself, lower your mask, share your truth, and enjoy time and experiences together. It's being in friendships or romances where you hold each other accountable and lift each other up—the mirror experience. This is how you grow even closer. "Connection for me," my client Sarah said, "is when I feel loved for who I am and who I am becoming."

Connection can be about seeking similarities (you both love movies or talking politics) and about appreciating differences (you enjoy cooking at home, and they enjoy ordering in; you prefer driving places, and they like taking an Uber; you like staycations, and they prefer vacations).

It's also the unconditional reciprocity of listening, talking, giving, and taking—trying to understand and to be understood. Connection can be quick and for only a moment in time; it can also be slow and last forever, often bringing us joy, laughter, comfort, and a fresh perspective.

"I don't tell very many people about every detail of my life, but I tell my journal."

Carrie Underwood
@carrieunderwood

Connection Is Not . . .

Connection is not conditional, superficial, one-sided, or out of balance. Connection isn't someone saying, "I'll love you when . . ." Undoubtedly, connection is hard work, but it shouldn't always be this way and you shouldn't be doing all the heavy lifting. If a specific "connection" sparks insecurity, loneliness, and fear in you, you may want to reconsider whether this connection is the right fit for you.

Connection is not feeling that you must hold back your words when you have something to say or pretending you are "fine" when you really are not.

Most of all, connection shouldn't hurt. You should feel boosted and bolstered, not criticized, condemned, or cut down.

"When people call me either a girl crush or their best friend, like, the best friend they want, that's, to me, the best compliment anyone could ever give me."

Mindy Kaling
@mindykaling

CONNECTION

Why Does Connection Matter?

Connection matters because we are hardwired for it. This means that we need connection to not only survive (think: safety in numbers) but thrive (think: how much you have benefited from a group of people who can relate to you with "me too.")

In their book, *Burnout*, Emily and Amelia Nagoski suggest that social connection is a form of nourishment, though these "nutritional" needs for connection change over our lifespans, unlike our need for food. "Our need for connection changes across our lifespans," they write, "but our fundamental need for connection does not."[25] What that means is that sometimes you may need a connection where you can enjoy wild, crazy, and outrageous fun, while at other times, your connection needs to be calmer, filled with tenderness, empathy, and understanding.

Feeling close and connected helps us feel physically and emotionally safe and secure. Belonging and fitting in simply feels good and what many of us look for.

When you connect with someone, the brain releases dopamine, and when you are hugged, the brain releases oxytocin, the bonding hormone. Closeness is an elixir, and naturally, we want even more. The expression "a little is good, more must be better" is the perfect phrase for relationships that are working well! Unfortunately, we don't always find healthy or helpful connections, as sometimes we give too much, receive too little, tolerate someone else's unhealthy ways, or are mistreated.

When you are less connected or not connected at all—perhaps you are connecting virtually but not in real time, or finding it hard to find the people who get you—you may experience loneliness and isolation. Sometimes you want to give up when it comes to relationships because they are too difficult, uncertain, or unstable. Perhaps, the connection feels forced or artificial, unfair, or off. Or you may be like Priya Parker who, in her book, *The Art of Gathering*, confides that "in my work, I strive to help people experience a sense of belonging. This probably has something to do with the fact that I have spent my own life trying to figure out where and to whom *I* belong."[26]

I once read an article in *The Wall Street Journal* called "The Lonely Burden of Today's Teenage Girls" that opened my eyes to the fact that, although the globe is more connected now than ever before, young women are also more solitary. According to the authors, "many girls spend their Saturday nights home alone, watching Netflix and surfing social media."[27] Not surprisingly, these girls also found themselves ill-prepared to navigate real-life activities, such as dating, working, and obtaining a driver's license. This article makes an excellent argument that, though times have changed, our human need for connection has not. Life is hard but is better when we are living it together.

You may be more outgoing or shyer, or you may have some social awkwardness or social acumen. You may have one friend or many. No matter. Connection is still vital to your happiness and healthfulness.

> "Connection is everything to me. I love spending time with people and getting to know their unique stories!"
>
> **Adrienne Chan**
> *@dr.adrienneacupuncture*

5 Ways to Nurture Connection

Decide on your relational must-haves.

Know the difference between healthy and unhealthy connections.

Find people who are similar to you and who are different from you.

Establish a strong and diverse support circle.

Connect in real time and in person.

What Blocks Connection?

Connection can be blocked by many things, but I find that among the young women I know and work with, what keeps them feeling disconnected are the secrets and lies they hold on to, the time they invest in toxic relationships, and the amount of energy they put into digital relationships over those in real time.

Secrets and Lies

I want to tell you some secrets: my parents got divorced when I was nine, but I didn't tell anyone until I was nineteen. And I was so lonely in my "single in the city" days that I seriously contemplated paying a company to match me with a mate.

I am sure you have secrets of your own. Maybe you don't want anyone to know how much you like listening to a certain music group, or maybe you once stole makeup from the mall. Or, more seriously, maybe you have been hiding your drinking, drugging, bingeing, or starving. Perhaps you are struggling to understand your sexuality and how you identify.

Secrets keep us feeling safe and secure, hidden from the possibility of being misunderstood, or worse, rejected, and sometimes, it's simply easier to keep our secrets than it is to share them. Secrets also make us feel shame and keep us feeling disconnected.

We also tell lies, sometimes white lies and half-truths to protect ourselves or avoid hurting others' feelings—like when you tell your friend you'd *love* to go to the party with her when what you *really* want is to sink into a bubble bath with a good book—and sometimes full-fledged lies, such as asking your professor for an assignment extension because you are "just polishing off your essay," when in reality, you haven't even started.

We feel that secrets and lies protect us from pain. Yet, they also keep us far from what we may really want: closeness. Maybe this idea will help: you cannot feel known by others if you do not show up and share who you are. Furthermore, you cannot possibly feel intimate (or "in-to-me," as my friend says) unless you are willing to take the chance to be vulnerable.

I know how it is much easier to put up thick walls. Yet, take it from me, when you take steps toward letting others know your quirks, hidden talents, fears, and dreams, you also let them into your secret world. I'm not saying let everyone in. Actually, the opposite: let no one in until you are certain and ready, but don't insist on impossible standards either.

What helped me become more vulnerable and more honest—which then allowed me to be known and to know others on a deeper level—was to practice "show and tell" and sharing stories or little pieces of who I am, really. That's right, the activity you may have learned in kindergarten can come in very handy here.

Practice one show and one tell at a time. A show could be a skill or talent, such as your natural gift of striking up conversations with complete strangers, or a quality, such as your fierce loyalty. A tell could sound like this: "Did I ever tell you about the time . . ." or "Today was a rough one, and I'd love to talk about it with you." Over time and with practice, you slowly show and share more of yourself. Over time, it gets easier.

Toxicity Tolerance

Now, you and I are going to take a little ride on a tandem bike. Together we are going to pedal our way through this section, and if at any time you feel uncomfortable, all you have to do is lift your feet off the pedals and let me keep pedaling. This section is tough and important. I'll start with a story of my own.

When I was working on my master's in education, I spent two consecutive summers living in San Diego. I was not looking for love, but I did find infatuation. His name was Ryan, and his confidence was refreshing. We went to the beaches, the movies, and the mall. I was into him. Then he started to scare me, snapping every so often to say that what I said was "ridiculous" or getting angry if I was a few minutes late for a date. Once he even left me in a store because I was browsing on my own.

I see now how unhealthy our connection was, but I did not see it at the time. When I returned home, my aunt, who knew I liked Ryan, told me this: "Nobody should ever make you feel scared." Her words stayed with me, and I broke it off with Ryan right away, without much explanation. As quickly as he entered my life, he exited. Phew!

It is my experience that some women tend to have what I am going to call a toxicity tolerance: an acceptance for toxic behaviors that can show up in subtle put-downs and undecipherable sarcasm or more severe treatment like gaslighting (when someone tries to make you question yourself). You may not see red flags, but you may *feel* them. People who try to change you, control you, or yell at you don't make you feel good. You can make excuses: "They didn't mean to yell" or "They are just really stressed right now." You may doubt yourself: "I was out of line by giving my opinion." But toxic is toxic and so damaging.

Consider a different kind of toxicity: Do you have friends who undermine you or make you doubt yourself? Maybe you are in a work group filled with gossipy or jealous people. If this is the case for you, I know it's difficult and unfathomable, but you need to make sure that your voice is heard and that they hear their behavior needs to change. You need to find the courage to leave the group if they refuse to change. You need to do a "spring cleaning"—decluttering your life of individuals who do not meet your need for healthy connection so that you can make room for those who do. You need to walk through any discomfort you anticipate, and although this is in no way easy, it is essential.

Maybe all you know is toxicity. Perhaps you come from a family where connection was marred by toxicity. Maybe this is your first relationship and you don't know better or don't have any relationship tools. Maybe you don't believe you deserve any different or any better. Perhaps you are thinking that your "good enough for right now" relationship or a no-strings attachment is what you want. Or perhaps you are deluding yourself into thinking this "wrong" person is actually the "right" person, despite your gut, friends, and family trying to tell you they're absolutely *not* "the one."

You are going to have to get really honest with yourself here. I remember someone telling me this once: "When you see crazy coming, cross the street." But what about when you don't see crazy coming, and you not only stay on that street but also start chasing crazy?

Toxic is toxic, so I am going to list all the toxic behaviors (most of which I have tolerated at some point) so you know what to look for. Remember, real and genuine connection feels good. These are signs of unhealthy connections:

- Controlling or manipulative
- Wanting to know where you are all the time
- Trying to change you
- Overly critical or overly demanding
- Showing jealousy and insecurity
- Physical or emotional abuse
- Putting you down or belittling you
- Cheating on you
- Yelling or screaming at you

There are also as many signs that someone is a healthy partner, and you need to pay attention to these signs as well. These are signs of healthy connections:

- Curious but not critical
- Lets you be yourself
- Accepting
- Encouraging but not pushing
- Kind and caring
- Unconditional loving
- Empathetic and understanding
- Seeks to know you
- Supportive
- Tells you all you can do
- Compliments
- Communicates

I want to take a minute here to ask you to choose one relationship you have and then go through these lists to evaluate whether this person is healthy (for you) or not healthy (for you). When we collect this kind of data, we can sometimes see truth more easily.

> **Note to Self**
>
> If you find yourself in an unhealthy and physically or emotionally abusive relationship, please tell at least one person, seek support now, and use the resources available in your community to give you both the information and the strategies for getting out. You are worth it, and you deserve better.

Digital vs. Real Connection

Virtual anything can not be real but *feel* real. Seriously, I *feel* I have hundreds of friends through my social platforms, but the inescapable reality is I don't. The ability to connect instantly to anyone does not equal real connection because something is missing. It's like eating a diet full of candy. In the moment, it satisfies, but later you are hungry, empty, and dissatisfied.

When I spoke with my clients about virtual dating and digital friendships, I expected them to be all for the online option, but they surprised me with a much more balanced view. Here are their thoughts and opinions on the subject captured in pros and cons.

Here are the pros of online relationships:

- Casual and informal (no pressure)
- Easy, fun, and convenient (less scary, awkward, or intimidating)

- A starting point or first step to more serious dating (can eventually meet in person, when ready)
- Testing the waters and experimenting with dating and meeting people eventually IRL with similar interests and hobbies
- Safe (can delete, block, report, or ghost if feeling uncomfortable, scared, or violated)
- An opportunity to find and connect with all kinds of people, all over the world (people they wouldn't meet otherwise), and experiment and explore socially
- Attention and validation

And here are the cons of online relationships:

- Doesn't always feel real (what you see is not what you get) or become anything more than superficial
- Can feel like a game (easy to lie about age, gender, personality, interests)
- Time consuming and addicting
- May feel worried when you don't receive communication back (ghosted)
- Overwhelming stress and worry can make you feel vulnerable and exposed
- Social media influencers can use you or deem you "invaluable" to them and unfollow you
- Unsafe: online creeps, predators, and harassers
- Promotes hookup culture
- Oversexualized images give way to a lack of body confidence
- Don't learn the social skills you can in person, such as how to express feelings, work through the tough stuff and fight fair, take criticism, and then become even more socially anxious

Connecting is critical to a sense of belonging and balance. When you find your people, you gain so much! You can easily grab a phone to connect via text, but online connection is still second best compared to the in-person kind.

Nurture connection with people who bring out the best in you.

What Builds Your Connection?

Connection is paramount to feeling included and even inspired. This doesn't mean that we are meant to connect with *all* humans or that *all* connection is healthy. That's why we need to look at how establishing boundaries and borders, keeping your friend circles eclectic, and connecting in real life can help you feel safe and supported emotionally, psychologically, and physically in all your relationships.

Boundaries and Borders

Early on in my company venture, Bold New Girls, I learned that young minds need creativity and fun to make abstract ideas more understandable. They needed tangibles, such as arts, crafts, and, yes, Hula-Hoops to better understand big ideas like relational boundaries.

That is why I showed up at one summer workshop with ten Hula-Hoops. I gave each girl one hoop and asked her to step inside as I explained that she needed to stand in the center, strong and confident. "This is your Hula-Hoop, nobody else's, and you can create this space for yourself and consider who and what you want and need inside and outside your circle." These girls got it, telling me they'd include play, fun, laughter, and nice girls who share. Excluded would be disgusting foods, homework, and mean girls.

Later, in my work with older girls and young women, the conversations around boundaries took a deeper turn. We talked about who and what they say yes and no to and how to do this effectively. Conversations about boundaries are difficult. I know how hard it is to not only set a boundary, especially when it comes to invitations and connections, but also keep a boundary, even when you are afraid of disappointing others or losing friends. So, we practiced what boundaries sound like, such as "yes, that works for me," "yes, that feels right," "no, I'm not available," or "no, I'm not interested." This question almost always follows that practice session: "But how do I know what boundaries to set and keep?"

A boundary feels right for you when you don't think about it a lot or second-guess yourself after you've set it. You will not even hesitate. Self-help experts often say it this way: "If it's not a hell yes, it's a no." My first client, Emily, who I am still in touch with, let me know that her recent hell yes was "incorporating meditation into my morning routine." Her hell no was "not letting negative people affect my own happiness." Of course, learning to trust yourself takes time and practice. The flip side is that not setting a boundary feels worse, energy zapping, stressful, and simply wrong.

Boundaries are the limits and lines that keep us safe and help us truly know what we want (and don't want), what matters most to us, and how we want others to treat us. Nedra Glover Tawwab, author of *Set Boundaries, Find Peace*, says that boundaries can be physical, emotional, intellectual, material, temporal, and sexual. The beauty of boundaries is this: they can be fluid and flexible as we grow. At the same time, boundaries need to become firm borders in more serious situations, such as when people take advantage of you or treat you in unacceptable ways. This is when your no needs to be a strong no!

Don't worry if you are not getting it right all the time. With every boundary you wanted to set and didn't, or set and then stepped over (yes, this happens), you are in a process of sorting out what your boundaries are. Boundaries change as you try new things, as you meet new people, and as your preferences change. There will be instances where you need to remind people of your boundaries. Whether we are talking personal space, conversation topics, or shared activities, your boundaries are *your* boundaries.

Years after the Hula-Hoop summer workshops, I ran into a mom of a young girl named Amelia. She told me this: "Lindsay, my daughter remembers your Hula-Hoop lesson well. There was a profound shift in her when you told her that she is not responsible for other people's Hula-Hoops, that she doesn't have to take care of other people's feelings or step into their hoops to help them. She can be in her hoop, separate and healthy, caring, and still set her own boundaries."

The Yes and No of Boundaries

When it comes to setting your boundaries, consider the following topics and what your boundaries might sound like.

Idea	Yes	No
Your time and availability	"Yes, I am available on short notice."	"No, I need a heads-up on plans."
Conversation topics	"Yes, I can talk about struggles and stresses."	"No, I cannot talk about my family stuff."
Activities and opportunities	"Yes, I can give that a try."	"No, that won't work for me at this time."
Changes and cancellations	"Yes, I am okay with a change in plans."	"No, I am not okay with changes, especially last-minute ones."
Apologizing	"Yes, I will be accountable for my mistakes."	"No, I will not over-apologize, especially for mistakes that are not mine."
Communication: time of day, type (Instagram, Snapchat, in-person) and frequency	"Yes, I can talk at night, in any way, and often."	"No, I can't talk after 10 p.m. I prefer texting, and every few days works for me."
Helping and giving	"Yes, I like to help out and give, and I like to be helped and to receive."	"No, I don't want to help or give more than is fair."
Lifestyle habits	"Yes, I am open to social drinking."	"No, I don't want to drink."

This lesson was echoed by Claire, who is in her late teens and who shared this with me: "Boundaries and borders are something that require adjusting as I meet new people and encounter new situations. Sometimes, I realize my boundaries are too soft and I agree to things I don't really want to do. Other times, my borders go up too quickly or they are too solid, and I know I have to give people a chance (or many chances) and be more flexible when circumstances change."

Keeping It Eclectic

"I am so thankful for my friends. Honestly, I just don't know where I'd be without the three girls I met in high school and who I have stayed close with throughout university and now into our early adult years," said Layla. "We have gone through *everything* together!"

Layla's long-lasting friendships are enviable to me. When I was trying to find my people in my late teens and early twenties, I was also watching TV shows like *Friends* and *Sex and the City*. Those TV shows were filled with people who met up regularly for coffee or martinis and who were always there for each other.

Despite my best efforts though, I was having trouble finding *my* people, and so I thought there was something wrong with me. Over time, tears, and complaints to my younger brother, he finally helped me see this truth: the groups of girls I wanted to join shared wine and gossip and neither of these pastimes were really me. He encouraged me to make my friend circle one that fit who I am. Brilliant!

I came to see there is no ideal formula for friendship—there is only *my way*. Here's what I knew: I didn't like big noisy groups. After time with people, I needed to recharge with "me time." I prefer the one-on-one connection—deep conversation over superficial chitchat. I appreciate being friends with many kinds of people: those like me, those unlike me, older and younger friends, girlfriends and boyfriends, friends for a reason, friends for a season, and forever friends.

Essentially, I created an eclectic circle of all types of friends: friends who I have fun with and keep things light; friends who are serious and inquisitive; those with shared interests and activities; others with crazy different ideas and innovations; friends with diverse cultural, religious, social, and educational backgrounds—a little bit of everyone and a lot of interesting and inspiring people. Since I know that different friends meet my different needs and I meet different friends' needs, I also know there must be some fluidity and flexibility when it comes to relationships.

Malina reminded me that relationships really are give-and-take. She said, "There are times, for me, that I feel there is so much going on for me; there is so much on my plate, I am constantly reaching out for friends' help and advice. I start to feel guilty and then remember that, when they need me, I am always there for them. I like that I am someone they can count on as we ebb and flow through our ups and downs."

Relationships can make life easier and better or harder and worse. They are a series of getting together, breaking up, making up, letting go, and starting all over again. You will be required to open your heart and feel all the feels, to trust and to have faith, to triumph and go through trying times together. The choice is always yours: more relationships or fewer or none, choosing to fly solo. It's your prerogative and your life. Not all humans match so find the people that are the best match for you: those who bring out the best in you!

The connections you make, whether we are talking friends, lovers, roommates, teammates, or life mates, all teach you something about yourself.

Unfortunately, some young women, like my client Carmen, aren't so much learning about themselves as they are losing themselves. Carmen met someone she enjoys being with, but she is worried that their love will fade or that she'll be cheated on. She tries to do everything right to make the relationship work and assumes that one false move will blow the whole thing up. Unfortunately, while she's protecting this connection, she is losing something valuable: herself. This is a red flag in a relationship.

My response to Carmen was to show her how healthy connections function using two circles and three types of connection.

The Distant Connection

You are two separate circles operating at a safe distance, often due to fear of being vulnerable.

The Too Close Connection

You are two overlapping circles with the exact same interests and opinions, with blurred boundaries, and no separation at all.

The Balanced Connection

You are two interconnecting circles with shared activities, conversations, and experiences but with separate activities as well. In this connection of "together and separate," there is more love than fear.

All of us have unmet needs for safety and security, love and belonging, connection and collaboration, but if we look to specific relationships to meet *all* those needs, we put pressure and even demands on the other person. Your personal work is to identify what your unmet needs are and try to meet them without leaning on other people all the time. This is transformative because then you can enjoy relationships instead of expecting others will give you exactly what you need when you need it.

Think deeply about all the kinds of relationships you can create. Choose people who help you feel hopeful, positive, and worthy; who build you up and allow you to be your unfiltered self; and don't make you feel guilty, ashamed, insecure, insignificant, or break you down.

Mixing It Up

Explore this list of friend characteristics and consider the kinds of people you include or would like to include in your friendship circle. The people you know are probably a mix of a few of these characteristics because none of us are caricatures. But often we gravitate to somebody for one characteristic or another. Think hard also about what kind of friend *you* are for others because friendship can only thrive when there is give-and-take.

- Delightfully different friend
- Problem solver
- Advice giver
- Spontaneous adventurer
- Empathetic listener
- Deep thinker
- Long-distance friend
- Life of the party
- Social advocate

Real Connection in Your Real World

Real connection may be in person or online. Occasionally I feel like the differences are becoming indecipherable. Yet, I can tell you that there is no replacing the presence of another—the experience in real time. And sometimes you need a little luck and a chance encounter.

One November morning I headed out to journal over coffee and then buy groceries. As I unloaded my food items, I felt a warm, calm energy emanating from the ever-so-attractive man in front of me who was paying for his groceries. I tried to get his attention to no avail. So, I asked the cashier, Aileen, "Who *was* that?" She explained that he came each Saturday morning. He was always polite and quiet. As far as she knew, he was also single.

As I left, my feet planted on the floor. I swear this was a moment of divine intervention. I went back to Aileen, gave her my business card, and told her to pass it on to our mystery man the next time she saw him. The very next day, I received the politest email of my life from the mystery man. He had returned to the store for milk the next day and went to his favorite cashier, Aileen, and she remembered to give him my card. He was intrigued by my company and me and wanted to meet for sushi (my favorite food) that week. Flash forward five years later, and we are happily connected.

Do we have a flawless connection? No way. We have had ups and downs and sideways moments, too. Never have I ever been so challenged to stretch myself, pushed to seek truth in myself and with others, and encouraged to become even more. Never have I ever felt so uncomfortable and then comfortable showing up as myself and relationally secure (most of the time). And we both put in relentless, unwavering effort to keep things strong.

Do you know people who expect connection to merely happen without any effort at all? Instead of being passive in relationships—online or in-person, serious or casual, long or short term, be the friend you want. If you want a caring friend, be caring; if you want a supportive friend, show your support; if you want a friend who knows you well, be known. If you want attention, give it! If you want affection, show it! If you want love, be love!

What I am trying to say is that, instead of looking for connection, be connection. Deliah said it best when she told me this: "I know I am the initiator in my relationships, and I am so proud of this—I create connections and connections happen!"

Nurturing Healthy Relationships

Nobody gets it right the first time. Here's a list of tips and tricks to help you cultivate healthy connections.

* Express yourself openly and honestly, and try to choose in-person chats over online: "I really need to tell you about . . ."
* Listen with your full attention, ask questions, and try not to steer the conversation toward yourself: "What was that like . . ."
* Share ideas and experiences to be more known and understood: "Did I ever tell you about the time I . . ."
* Make connections such as: "I feel that way, too, sometimes" or "I'm glad I am not the only one."
* Use your powers of observation and curiosity to notice changes: "You seem to be excited/stressed today. What's going on?"
* Compliment work (if not too excessive) and focus on strengths and positive qualities: "I really appreciate how you let me tell my whole story without interrupting" or "I love your new outfit."
* Consider balance in giving and taking, in particular when it comes to conversation, making plans, or paying/treating.
* Discover; don't make assumptions when there are misunderstandings or no-show meetups: "Let me know what happened . . ."
* Fight fair; own your part (it takes two), find a good time to talk, share your experience (use "I" statements), ask for what you need (don't demand), assure the person you want to figure this out, listen, and compromise on a solution: "I have a concern I want to bring up; is now a good time?"
* Do not cut all communication or ghost people when you feel hurt, mad, or disappointed. Instead, try feeling your feelings and deciding when and how to express yourself.

MADE FOR MORE

Self-Interview

What does connection mean to you?

How do you create and maintain connection in relationships?

What are some obstacles when it comes to connection?

How do you work through times of disconnection to become even more connected to someone?

What makes connection "easy" or "difficult" for you?

People and relationships can be confusing. I am not going to say cultivating connection and maintaining it isn't a lot of hard work, and sometimes I wonder if it's worth it—the baffling and bewildering behavior of humans being, well, human. Glennon Doyle, author of *Untamed* among other books, says, "I am a sensitive, introverted woman, which means that I love humanity but actual human beings are tricky for me."[28] To that I say yes!

Georgia shared with me how connection can be both confusing and rewarding. She said, "My childhood friend Natasha and I grew up together building tree forts, having sleepovers, going to our first school dances, and sharing late night chats. She always said she'd be there for me no matter what. You know, BFFs. But when I was bullied in high school by the mean girl gang, not only did her actions not match her words but she joined the gang and used my deepest secrets as ammunition against me. I was so hurt and learned that, though I loved having the connection with Nat, I had to figure out who will really be there for me in the good times and the tough times, through their words *and* their actions!"

Connection can remind us of who we truly are and show us the parts of ourselves we forget or dismiss. At the same time, people can baffle and bewilder you as much as they interest and fascinate you. Connecting with others can help us think, feel, dream, heal, and become better people. We need food, air, and water, and we also need the love we can find in authentic connection.

MADE FOR MORE

To be honest . . .

What could a fresh start on connection mean to you?

CONNECTION

The More and Less of Connection

More...

* Love in all kinds of ways
* Laughter and joy
* Time together
* Interesting conversations
* Discovering places, people, and life
* Variety of relationships
* Letting go of unfit or unhealthy connections

Less...

* Fighting
* Trying to find "ideal" relationships
* One type of relationship
* Superficial connections
* Expectations of how connection *should* be
* Forcing connections that aren't there
* Game playing

Chapter 7
More Power, Less Fear

To be honest . . .

Do you feel undeserving of power?

Do you worry you will never feel powerful?

Do you feel intimidated by powerful people and hold back?

Do you admire inspiring people but think "that will never be me"?

Do you let fear take over your desire for more passion and purpose?

Find your power. Know your power. Be powerful.

I have a secret superpower. My superpower has nothing to do with striving to be rich or successful. It's not related to my social media platforms or my social circles. It has everything to do with who I am—on the inside. My superpower is powerful. Do you want to know what my secret superpower is? My sparkle and shine. I've had it since I was little. My sparkle will not be stifled. Truth be told, sometimes I can't sleep or eat or do anything else because I am too excited and enthusiastic about all that I can create, offer, and contribute to this world. This superpower sparkle is the result of my passion, purpose, and power.

I see this same sparkle in young women like Camilla, who is passionate about helping people as an elementary school teacher. She doesn't see her power in the classroom as a way to control her students, colleagues, or parents but rather as a way to bolster them. She works tirelessly, focusing on solutions instead of complaining about systems (educational or others) that are old or broken. Admittedly, she said she cares too much what others think of her and how this can hinder her movement forward, but ultimately, she knows she is a human *in progress* who is committed to stewarding her power for the greater good.

So far, we have explored your happiness, confidence, authenticity, progress, mindfulness, and connection. As you work on strengthening these essential qualities, you'll find that you are better able to tap in and grow into your own power. For Camilla, this means "living your life from a place of power to make the world around you a better place." But living your life from a place of positive power can show up differently in different individuals. Unlike Camilla, Maddy describes her power as being more subtle. She makes time to "do really simple things as I move throughout my day, like smiling or buying people coffee. One time, I even got into a conversation with some lost tourists about the city and gave them some ideas for their adventures."

Take a moment to think about how your power is showing up in your life as you read through this chapter. What is *your* superpower?

What moves your heart most becomes your most passionate source of power.

What If? Then What?

What if **you believed all the power you needed was inside of you?** ▸ *Then would you feel clearer about your purpose?*

What if **you put this power into practice every day?** ▸ *Then would others see just how powerful you can be?*

What if **your power was something you never gave up on?** ▸ *Then would you be able to persevere, especially when things got hard?*

What if **you embraced the examples that the powerful women set for us all?** ▸ *Then would you say "I can do this, too"?*

What if **you saw power not as prestige but as your calling?** ▸ *Then would you feel compelled to make a difference?*

What Is Power?

Power is inside of you. Seriously. Power is a feeling of inner strength and confidence, yes, but also of unwavering passion and conviction. When you know you are powerful, you are much more willing to be bold and brave, even badass, take chances, make changes, and do what you want and also what is right. People say that with great power comes great responsibility, so be responsible for putting your power to good use. Speak up for yourself and others, speak your mind, stand up for truth, and stand up for others and causes that matter to you. When things get tough, your power will help you keep going instead of holding back or giving up.

Connecting with your power is knowing that you have a point, a place, and a purpose on this planet—and you will think big, without limits, and not only open doors but walk right in because you can. Power allows you to say "I can do anything!" Power is figuring out what's next when you have no idea which way to go, finding energy when you are running on empty, and fighting for those on issues that matter and for those who cannot fight for themselves. Your power gives you street cred.

Power Is Not . . .

Power is not about control, manipulation, or abusing your position. It is not about pleasing others or caving into pressure to maintain the status quo. Power is not about taking the easy way out or waiting for change to happen. Nor is it about feeling underestimated or allowing fear to prevent you from doing the things you need and want to do.

Power has nothing to do with sidestepping struggle, coming up with reasons why you can't participate, turning away from truth, or avoiding the discomfort found in changing what's not working.

Power has everything to do with not letting your critics, or a bad day, win but instead deciding to keep going.

Why Does Power Matter?

I told you about my fresh start at the beginning of this book (see page 7)—my decision to quit my job in my early thirties. This was probably the most powerful fresh start I'd made up to that point in my life, and it helped me clarify all that I was thinking about in my twenties about making change. I share this story with you, even though you may still be in college or just starting your career, to show you that fresh starts are available to you, now and later. This is a tool you can use whenever you find your power dissolving because it will allow you to take charge of your life again.

I gave my notice on a Tuesday, and by Wednesday, I had received several nasty emails. There were closed-door meetings that I was not invited to attend. My work colleagues hadn't anticipated me leaving. However, I was visibly unhappy with a work environment in which I felt undervalued, underappreciated, and overlooked for my potential. Many small companies don't have the safety net of a human resources department, so I was on my own, fighting this battle.

When my boss kept pushing me to reconsider my decision, making it seem I didn't have the right to quit, something happened inside of me. I felt increasingly uncomfortable with the pressure—it felt so powerfully wrong in my body. So, I decided to quit right then and there. I told my boss that I did not have to put up with the pressure. "Your behavior right now is unacceptable. I am leaving," I said. With that, I walked out the door and never looked back. If you had told me that morning this was going to happen, I wouldn't have believed you, and yet there I was, standing tall and strong, devoid of any signs of trepidation and 100 percent certain this was the right decision for me. I knew my power mattered at that moment.

These standout, powerful moments aren't always frequent. But feeling your power can arrive in everyday moments as well. For example, you may feel powerful when you meet a personal best on a run, ask for a raise, show off your thrifty fashion find, or decide that your health will be your priority from now on. These are all examples of powerful moments.

Even if you don't feel powerful right now, know how essential it is for you to be powerful. When you know you are powerful, something changes inside of you. Sometimes the impetus for a power moment is anger, something so unjust, you must speak up and act. Sometimes, the motivator is passion—you believe in an idea, a person, or a cause so deeply that you know you have to be part of it.

These power moments will lead you to pay more attention, to focus on what matters most to you, to learn and grow, to show up and help, to discover your deepest desires, to contemplate creative solutions to problems, or to defy the status quo. Most of all, they reveal your purpose. You know what else? They will change how you influence the world around you. Is it strange to point out the obvious here, but your power is, well, powerful!

I hear my clients tell me, "But I am just one person. How much power do I really have?" Think of it this way: "I am one person. How much power do I want to hold?" Power is a limitless resource ready and waiting for you to believe in and tap into. See what you can make happen with each thought you choose and each action you take. In the words of Sophia Amoruso, founder and former CEO of Girlboss: "You combine hard work, creativity, and self-determination, and things start to happen. And once you start to understand that alchemy, or even just recognize it, you can begin to see the world in a different way."[29] You also begin to play around with possibilities of what or all you can do!

Note to Self

Many of us learned to be kind and courteous and to avoid expressing anger. Yet, I am here to tell you that sometimes your anger need not be held back because it can tell you something important needs your attention. Yes, your anger can easily cause you to explode, overreact, and act without thinking. But, when checked and expressed in a healthy way, anger is the feeling you may need to propel you into action and advocacy.

5 Ways to Promote Power

Keep growing yourself.

Surround yourself with powerful influencers.

Seek out inspiration every day.

Do what matters most to you.

Think and dream even bigger.

What Can Block Power?

Most young women I work with don't even consider that they can be powerful. I may reflect how they are growing in strength and power. For example, I told Joanne she was powerful when she decided to tell her parents she was genderflux. I helped Michelen see her power was growing in her ability to set boundaries with friends who always flaked out on plans. I reminded Tia that her power was her ability to use her negative life experience growing up in an unsafe home to better relate to her friends and others who were struggling. The reasons they were unable to see and feel their own power can be traced back to these two ideas: a faulty belief system and outdated power structures.

A Faulty Belief System

Let's say you want to build your dream house. What would happen if you constructed your home on a wobbly foundation? You guessed it—your house would be unstable. This is no different from you building beliefs on a faulty belief system.

You may be operating from a framework of self-doubt and a lack of self-worth. This is an old and flawed belief system that doesn't help you grow or feel powerful in any way. If you can take the leap and let go of these old beliefs, you can make room for new and much more powerful beliefs.

In his book *Think Again*, Adam Grant explains that we all have values and beliefs and that it's wise to challenge our beliefs and adapt new ones as we change and grow. In other words, don't hang on to any one idea too tightly because, when you rethink your beliefs, you become even more of who you want to be and even more powerful. So true!

Right now, your belief system may sound like "I don't deserve power" or "I'll never get what I want." But if you want to tap into and grow your own power, your belief system needs to sound like this: "I am more than enough," "Of course, I can," "Yes, me," and "I can do this."

To let go of your old narratives, you need to create new ones. Here's a trick that the women I work with use. We create a new narrative as though it's already happened.

- I am now a graduate, working with a top-ranked law firm, living in the city, and spending weekends home decorating.
- After traveling abroad, I chose to join a nonprofit, supporting women who are starting up small businesses with micro loans.
- I'm pursuing my songwriting and training my puppy.
- I am living with my four friends in a townhome off campus as we all find balance between our studies and our part-time jobs.
- I graduated from technical college, and I am officially an electrician.
- I am dating and may have found a great person who is showing me how loyal and supportive they are.

Outdated Power Structures

I'll never forget the shocking realization that my male counterpart was earning five dollars more per hour than I earned at my first teaching job. Fuming and fearless, I confronted my *female* boss only to be told it was because "he had a family to support." Apparently, I was at a double disadvantage for being female and single.

Unfortunately, pay inequity and gender discrimination still exists today. We see this outdated system play out in so many social stereotypes, from positions of power to toxic words and phrases like "man up," "mansplaining," and "boys don't cry." Beyoncé sings about girls and women with power, but James Brown's song "It's a Man's Man's Man's World" reminds us that the patriarchy is alive and well. I want the world Queen Bey sings about.

Women are challenging the status quo and fighting for change. In the past we can look to Harriet Tubman, who led slaves to freedom, or suffragettes fighting for the right to vote. Today, we have modern-day warriors like Tarana Burke, founder of the #metoo movement; Swedish environmental activist Greta Thunberg; Pakistani activist Malala

Yousafzai; and US politician Alexandria Ocasio-Cortez (AOC). Women are speaking up more and stepping into leadership roles. Now, more than ever, there is more diversity in legislatures, more women receiving equal pay, and more women speaking up and standing up for what is right and fair. The tech sector is attracting more women to ensure technology is developed from a balanced perspective, and the emergence of female leaders is becoming a force of good in the world. After all, as W.E.B. Du Bois said and Dorothy Dandridge reiterated: "There is no force more powerful than a woman determined to rise."

There's so much to unpack here, but I'd need another book to do it in! What I most want to focus on in this book is creating awareness around what you may have to deal with through your young adulthood. Young women are deeply affected by outdated power structures and outmoded expectations of how they should behave. For example, have you ever been called "too" of anything? Too loud, too proud, too assertive, too confident, too smart, too social, too outspoken, too opinionated, or too ambitious? You are definitely not alone, and the struggle is real. People who are leading outdated power structures want to protect their position. Some of them will say things to make us doubt our ideas, question our abilities, and second-guess our plans.

My advice is that you surround yourself with people who encourage you to celebrate your accomplishments. Don't expect others to offer praise or accolades for your job well done, but be your own stamp of approval. And challenge any person who tries to block your power with this secret weapon: powerhouse messages. Replace each doubtful thought (whether it is yours or another person's) with a powerful countermeasure. Here are some examples:

- Why me? ▸ Why not me?
- They say I can't. ▸ Watch me.
- What will people think of me? ▸ Who cares what they think!
- It's been done before. ▸ I will do it in a new way.
- It's too hard to fight. ▸ I have to keep fighting.
- I am not strong enough. ▸ I will find the strength inside of me.
- Change feels scary. ▸ I will be brave.

Be courageous enough to speak up, stand up, and stand out!

What Builds Your Power?

Your power can be cultivated by embracing your passion and clarifying your purpose (the power of knowing what matters most to you). Foundational support comes from your ability to get moving (and maintain momentum) as well as your understanding of money management. Let's explore each of these ideas to empower you.

Embrace Your Passions to Clarify Your Purpose

When I started to listen to my heart and decided what I really wanted to do—help girls and young women grow and become confident and strong—I knew I had found my passion. It is all I could think, talk, and dream about. As I stepped into this truth, I began to feel that this was *me*, exactly what made me happy and exactly what I was supposed to be doing. Together, my heart and my actions gave me this unique sense: power. Why do I call it power? This is because it was my truth, my certainty, and the one thing that was inside of me that nobody could take away. When you step into your power, you become unstoppable.

Passion

Passion is what you love to do. But I suggest this: love many things. When you discover your passions (yes, more than one), you tap into a source of pure joy, a place where you are immersed and in flow—you don't even notice the clock ticking. Passion is what you most think about, talk about, and dream about doing in every spare moment.

But how do you know what your passions are? The easy answer is this: you take time to discover, to explore many different interests and activities, and you start to sort them into what you are most and least passionate about. Let's say for example that you think you want to become a better swimmer, but after just a few times in the pool, you realize you hate being trapped in a pool. Hiking and feeling free in nature are more your jam. Perhaps your whole life people have always told you that "you should be a politician—you are such a great speaker." So, you trust their insights and you try running for a position on your college student union. You surprise yourself by winning, and you quickly realize you love it so much. You wonder, "Why didn't I do this before?"

If you aren't sure what you are passionate about now, sometimes it helps to think about what you were into as a child: building things or organizing neighborhood games or whatever you were involved in during high school, whether that's drama, chess, coding, or law.

Follow whatever piques your curiosity as a young adult. When you are speaking with people, listening to news radio, searching for articles, or browsing a bookstore, what are the topics that grab you? Whatever they are—food, politics, education, astronomy, medicine, or sports—they are likely your passions.

My clients often come in telling me (or showing me) what they are most into. Jordan is often talking about her interest in gaming and app development. Shamma often arrives to our monthly sessions in her workout gear and talks about what running or biking event is coming up next for her. And Ayçe is by far the most musical person I know. I swear she knows every type of music and artist from the blues and Motown to modern day rock and roll!

Passions can often come from our pain, something that bothers you so much you feel a need to improve an experience for others. Other times, your passions can come from your enthusiasm about an idea, such as climate change or your ancestry. Your pains and your joys can become your "thing."

Here's something for you to try: if you are not yet clear on how to find your passion, write down a list of ideas or things you'd like to try—anything and everything—and take one month to try each idea. After thirty days, ask yourself what felt the most like you. Do more of those activities, ditch the ones you liked least, and replace these with other ideas. You just never know what new passions you might uncover!

Purpose

Purpose is what helps you get out of bed each morning, makes you want to stay up late into the night, makes you feel excited and motivated, puts a smile on your face, and lights you up and honors your self-worth. It's a bit like passion that way. Living a purposeful life is one with meaning, contribution, and fulfillment.

One of the most common questions I get from young women is this: "How do I find my purpose?" This is a valid question, especially since many are just graduating or wanting to transition from a simple job that pays the bills to that first step on their chosen career ladder.

Let me remove the pressure right now. You don't need to decide what your purpose is today. It's unrealistic to expect that your purpose will instantly align with your beliefs and values. And avoid basing your purpose on what someone else is doing or assuming that your purpose will last throughout your lifetime.

My purpose to empower girls and young women to feel happy, healthy, and confident was the result of pursuing my passions for creativity, health, fitness, learning, and personal growth, as well as some anger that girls were less confident than I felt they should be! Now, I show up for young women with a treasure chest filled with all my passions, which keep me interested, relevant, and valuable!

Every time I meet with Isla, she reminds me how far we have come together. "Remember when I couldn't tell you one thing I liked? And now, I can tell you *exactly* what I am passionate for, without any doubts at all: fashion, business, and of all things, cooking!" Yes, of course I remember. It took a lot of questions ("What do you love to do?"), time ("Isla, this takes how long it takes"), and trial-and-error growing ("Not into writing? That's okay. How about we explore home decorating?").

With less pressure to find your purpose *now*, you can let go of fear—fear of failing or failing to find purpose. Some common fears that my clients share with me are "How will I know for sure if this is my actual purpose?", "What if I settle and miss out on my purpose?", and "What if I never find my purpose, then what?" Fear doesn't help this process of finding purpose, but it does need recognition so that you can question it.

So often, fear is based on false premises, so now is the time to think like a scientist and collect your data. Here's how to do that.

- Think about your current ideas around your purpose and be willing to rethink when new information arrives.
- Embrace doubt and pursue more clarity.
- Be curious and ask questions.
- Accept that you will make mistakes and change your mind.

I want to share a quick example of someone who has discovered their purpose. My client Kayla is often found riding her bike or trail running after which she'll eat her oat and fruit parfait and feel ready to conquer her day! Initially Kayla went away to college to study kinesiology, but as she was nearing graduation and setting up her own company selling oatmeal cookies on Instagram, she learned how much she loved business. Now, she is working full-time at a health-focused eatery in the city where she is combining her passions for fitness, nutrition, business, and body movement.

"I believe we must know who we are if we're ever going to discover what we are made to do."

Jordan Lee Dooley
@jordanleedooley

Your Purpose Plan

When my client McKenna arrived at my workspace, she was dazed and confused about figuring out what to do with the "rest of my life." McKenna was an all-heart kind of girl, so we decided to use her strength (her feelings) to develop her area of growth (her thinking). Together we worked on creating a purpose plan for her. Check out this example and then make it your own.

Idea to Explore	How I Feel About This	The Outcome
Taking a bartending course (mixology)	Excited to try something new	Loved it more than I thought and applied for bartending jobs
Volunteering at the library	Happy about giving back	Enjoyed being part of the community
Going back to school to take a library science course	Uncertain if this is the degree I want	Got accepted into the college and I start in September
Working on my print designs	Enthusiastic about creating	Sold my first print on Etsy

"Let's Get Moving"

Your power will never "just happen." What you need is motivation and momentum, but you will need to be patient and take it one step at a time. I understand that you may feel unprepared and not ready, but you absolutely can move into your power.

There is a common misconception that you need motivation before you move. Not true. Actually, when you start moving, you create momentum. The more you move, the more momentum you generate. Starting is likely the most difficult part of moving as we focus on how difficult a task will be or how unsure we are that it will be worth our time and effort. Yet, there is tremendous power in the first step. So how do you start?

You need energy, and this begins with self-care. You need to ensure you are getting enough food, sleep, water, and time to revitalize. You know what else gives you energy? Eliminating time drainers such as the takers, who are critical and complain, and the time wasters, like spending too much time online or too much effort focusing on your problems and what's not working in your life. You will have to let go because you need more of your energy to get going and get giving. You need to also tap into your internal guidance system or power source, whether that's the universe, nature, God, or people who believe in you and want the best for you. Whatever your source, seek it and keep replenishing your beliefs.

"The best thing we could do is work as hard as we can for what is right and what is good."

Alexandria Ocasio-Cortez

@aoc

Creating Powerful Momentum

Momentum is created with each action you take. The point is to do something and then keep doing many more "somethings." A journey begins with a single step, so take that first step, then take another, and see what happens. My guess is that you will start to feel a shift in your energy, enthusiasm, and of course, outcome. Start with small daily steps that make a difference. Here are some ideas about how to do that:

* If you are concerned about climate change, take action by reducing your waste, recycling your water bottles, and reusing your clothes via donations.
* If you want to go to graduate school but lack the funds, start researching and applying for scholarships that might assist you in your academic goals.
* If you are feeling the burden of your family's dysfunction, ask your doctor if they offer counseling services as part of their practice.

Control Your Finances, Control Your Life

Every so often an email pops up from a proactive parent that says this: "Help! Can you coach my daughter on money management skills?" This is always an immediate hell yes for me! Here's the key thing you need to know: increased awareness and management of money matters mean decreased stress, worry, and debt.

When I'm coaching young women on money management skills, I typically start with some questions about money and specifically how they feel about money. Some feel excited and happy about money; others feel anxious, guilty, or confused. Then I zero in on their core beliefs about money. I give them the following list of statements and ask them to choose the one that sounds most like them.

- I never have enough money.
- I don't know how to save or invest.
- I don't deserve money.
- I'd rather not think about money.
- I am not very responsible with money.
- I waste and overspend my money.

Identifying their core beliefs helps them understand their current relationship with money. From here we look at three key parts of money: making it, spending it, and saving it.

Most young women I know are either looking for work or working already. Their job may be part-time or full-time or a series of jobs such as dog walking, house sitting, jewelry making, photography, or content creation. Some young women make money from being social media influencers (or micro influencers) with paid sponsorships and their own social media channel (this is not as easy or as quick as it seems; in fact, social media success can take years). Multiple streams of income may provide you with power of choice, and regardless of how you generate income, what's most important is that you are earning money.

Spending money is a hot topic because many of us underestimate how much we spend and we spend more than we have. This is why tracking your expenses is such a powerful habit. Some people use a spreadsheet, and others an app on their phones. When I coach young women on their spending habits, I ask them to consider whether a purchase is a need or a want, a priority or a luxury, so they develop their power of discernment—as in "Do I really need this?"

Usually, my favorite part of these coaching sessions on money management is the part where we talk about saving. We take what they are making and subtract what they are spending. The balance is what they have to save or even invest. Then they get to decide how to save—this could be a separate account or locked into a term deposit (ask your bank about this if you need to). They could also divide this amount into a few accounts, choosing to give 10 percent to a favorite charity or put 20 percent away for a rainy day or a just-in-case fund, or they may even decide to save for a bigger purchase like a car or condo—the power of preparing for their future.

Typically, I see young women light up when they understand that they have the capability of getting what they want with their hard-earned money as long as they are disciplined. Sonja shared with me her best money trick: putting small amounts of money into multiple accounts to save for specific items (in her case, it was a new iPad), and she beamed with happiness when she had saved enough.

The power that comes with this truth is priceless. And it doesn't just have to be about earning money and saving. You can gain just as much power from paying off your student loan debt as you can from saving to purchase your first car or condo. Trust me, this is a powerful confidence booster!

"Discover and embrace your unique personality, passions, and purpose, which in and of itself is powerful!"

Milissa Ewing
@maewing

Get in the Habit

To help you improve your money matters, I suggest you commit to taking on one habit at a time. Once the habit is yours, add the next.

* Pay attention to your money—what you earn, spend, and save.
* Don't spend more than you have.
* Know the difference between a want and a need.
* Save first, then spend.
* Make a monthly budget and stick to it.
* Decide how you will divide your savings.
* Talk to a financial advisor about different investment options.

POWER

Self-Interview

> What is an example of when you felt powerful and powerless?

> How did you discover your passions?

> What advice can you give someone wanting to know their purpose but feeling lost or overwhelmed?

> Who do you feel are role models that exude power? What is it that you see in them that is "powerful"?

> In what ways are you trying to be more powerful in your life?

Sometimes I feel a little dull and flat. So, every day I lean on my faith, and I pray: "God, please help me to keep doing what makes me sparkle so I can use my sparkle to help others." That's it, it's that simple, and the "more" of my faith. My purpose is to influence people in positive ways. My sparkle is my superpower, and my superpower is my purpose—every single day. Since helping young women is my purpose, it seems only natural to end with the power of their voices.

Asherita, who has just graduated with her law degree, knows that understanding her life's purpose is a nonlinear process that can change unexpectedly. For example, she said, "I had so many curveballs thrown at me during university. However, I was able to find meaning in every opportunity coming my way, and because I was open to change, the new experiences brought me new purpose." She's not kidding when she says she had curveballs to negotiate. While she was at university, her dad lost his job and her family experienced serious financial hardship. Asherita struggled to stay in school because she felt compelled to move home to help out. At her parents' insistence, she stayed in school and her family experience clarified what she wanted to focus on in her law studies. She chose to focus on employment law to help people like her dad feel more protected and supported.

Gabby, now a first responder, recognized at age twenty-one her power when she realized that the titles she used to introduce herself to others—student, girlfriend, manager—were reflective of outside sources of power. "My power was inside of me the whole time I was searching—my bottomless empathy, my compassion, and my love for helping others," she said. Now, Gabby tells people her name, and with every introduction, she reminds herself of who she is to herself without needing to prove herself to others or be defined by any label.

Always one to struggle with "comparisonitis," especially when it comes to her two sisters, twenty-two-year-old Emma always felt a silent pressure to keep up with her ambitious siblings. It took a lot of self-work for her to accept that she is different and on a different path from anyone else. She is neither academically inclined nor is she entrepreneurial, but she is socially adept, which is why she is a perfect fit for the hospitality industry. Emma says it's "all too easy to lose sight of your personal power, strengths, and career and life goals, so I've learned to constantly remind myself that I am exactly where I am supposed to be!" She tried to follow the path of others, then realized the only path she needs to follow is her own. You can follow your own path, too. Just create and design the more and less in your own life to make a fresh start today!

MADE FOR MORE

To be honest . . .

What could even more power mean to you?

The More and Less of Power

More . . .

* Self-belief
* Resiliency
* Believing in your power
* Surrounding yourself with people who believe in you, too
* Joining the table
* Making your voice heard
* Perspective taking
* Collective activism

Less . . .

* Self-doubt
* Giving up
* Thinking of other women as being more powerful than you
* Surrounding yourself with people who are jealous or critical of your new, powerful self
* Solo activism

A Letter to Yourself

When we began this adventure, I promised you two things: I'd tell you the truth and we'd do this together. Now, we are at the end of this book, and I hope you have a deeper understanding of your truth. I also hope you feel ready to try out some new ideas on your own.

My last ask, I promise, is one for you: write a letter to yourself about the promises you want to make and keep, what you are wanting and willing to change, and what you are most excited for. These are your pages to be real and raw as you end this book and begin your own journey.

Last Thoughts

Can you believe we are at the end of our time together? I am so proud of you for seeing this journey through the seven chapters to the end. Now, I have some last thoughts to share.

Today is your fresh start! I never want you to feel like you are not smart enough, worthy enough, talented enough, or ready enough. I always want you to feel equipped and empowered to make changes, big and small, to commit to your growth and development and to create the dreams you have and to build the life you really want. I want you to feel more than enough. I know change can feel scary, but hard doesn't mean change is impossible. I believe you can do amazing things with each small change you choose.

Trust yourself. Believe in yourself. Remember the pivotal "what if?" question to try: What if you could let go of your yesterday? What if you could take just one step forward? What if you could step into the new and more happy, confident, authentic, mindful, connected, and powerful you? Then what?

See your life as an unending chance to explore and experiment all you want more and less of, especially when it comes to thoughts, habits, choices, changes, adventures, activities, and ways of becoming. Using the solid foundation of good enough, more than enough, and all the self-belief and confidence you've accessed, I hope you will keep growing in the way you need. I also hope that you feel ready to embrace fresh starts in every aspect of your life.

Start with one—one push-up, one page, one habit, one promise, one thought, one idea, one goal. Start today. Repeat tomorrow. You are more than who you were. You can start over anytime, like today. Today is your fresh start, and every day that follows. You can keep starting fresh. You can write your new story.

With love and appreciation,

—Lindsay xo

Acknowledgments

In recent years, I have felt a tremendous sense of gratitude. So much so, I even bought myself a gold bangle bracelet and had it engraved with a heart and the words *forever grateful*. My life hasn't felt easy by any stretch of the imagination, but I do feel so thankful now for the life I have created and the life I get to live. That being said, there are so many people to thank!

I am forever thankful to God for the ideas, inspiration, humility, and even moments of discomfort—all infused into this book. I am forever thankful that I believe in God and that I'm reminded daily of His love, His grace, and His goodness. I know that He gave me the self-belief, the strength, and the wisdom to make this work reflect my true, authentic self every day.

I also want to thank some pretty special people: those who said not just yes but hell yes when I asked them to join me in the creation and collaboration of *Made for More*. They didn't hesitate (not a bit), and they showed me they were *all in* from the start. Do you know how exciting this was for me? Very!

I am so grateful for the team who has now supported me in writing three books, namely Maggie Langrick, who became genuinely excited when I pitched my concept to make this book more creative, colorful, and unique. Thank you, Allison Serrell, for your guidance, wisdom, and of course, expertise. To my editor, Sarah Brohman, who yet again seemed to "get me" and consistently offered her insights and wisdom throughout the entire writing and editing process, who held space for me to talk out and develop my ideas, and who encouraged and then drew out all my stories. Thank you, Jesmine, for always supporting me in so many ways. You are efficient and kind and I so appreciate this about you. To Morgan—you captured the essence with your creative flair and made this book come alive through your images and design.

To my family, especially my parents, who taught me both by example and also counterexample—I appreciate you. A special thanks to my mom for being my very first reader and championing me, and to my dad for weekly check-ins on my progress. To my friends, thank you for allowing me to be a little crazy yet always authentically me. You all really do mean a lot to me. I know I am a joyful, productive person and probably always will be. Now that this book is complete, I will have more time for you all. (That is, until the next creative idea!) Thank you for supporting me in small ways (happy thoughts, prayers, and quick calls) and bigger ways (reminding me of just how far I have come, why I do what I do, and all that makes me who I am today).

Kelvin, your strength and confidence, coupled with your belief in me, helped see this project through from beginning to end with surprisingly little stress and struggle. Thank you for always making time to hear my very early morning creative ideas. You keep my life real and truthful. You keep my life simple. You keep my life balanced. You make our life together an amazing adventure, every single day. I couldn't adore you more.

Thank you to all the authors, writers, designers, and creators for your books, articles, videos, and social media feeds, whose ideas both influenced me and inspired me. Thank you as well to my support circle who encouraged and championed me, including Tiffani, Brittany, Kelly, Mel, Adrienne, Amanda, Moyin, Alvin, and Dan. I needed your support in various ways at various times and you showed up for me.

Finally, I want to thank all the young women—those of you I know and those of you I have yet to meet. I know you have the potential to become even more—even more confident, even stronger, and even more authentically you. As you push further into the adult years, as you grow more secure in yourself, and as you learn your own lessons, please remember this: now more than ever, the world needs you. You, just as you are, have a purpose, and you, just as you are, can be your boldest, brightest self.

Notes

1. Karianne Gomez, Tiffany Mawhinney, and Kimberly Betts, "Welcome to Generation Z" (London: Network of Executive Women and Deloitte), deloitte.com/content/dam/Deloitte/us/Documents/consumer-business/welcome-to-gen-z.pdf.

2. Sarah Sladek and Josh Miller, "Ready or Not, Here Comes Z" (Richmond, VA: XYZ University, January 2018), xyzuniversity.com/wp-content/uploads/2018/08/Ready-or-Not-Here-Comes-Z-Final.pdf.

3. "What Is Happiness?" Psychology Today, psychologytoday.com/ca/basics/happiness.

4. Taylor Bennett, "What Is Positive Psychology? How Can This Movement Benefit Me?" Thriveworks, last modified November 20, 2018, thriveworks.com/blog/positive-psychology-movement-benefits.

5. Dan Baker and Cameron Stauth, *What Happy People Know: How the New Science of Happiness Can Change Your Life for the Better* (New York: Rodale, 2003), 37–38.

6. Kate Hudson, *Pretty Happy: Healthy Ways to Love Your Body* (New York: Dey Street Books, 2016), xix.

7. Michael Strahan and Veronica Chambers, *Wake Up Happy: The Dream Big, Win Big Guide to Transforming Your Life* (New York: Atria, 2015), 7.

8. Amanda MacMillan, "Why Instagram Is the Worse Social Media for Mental Health," *Time*, May 25, 2017, time.com/4793331/instagram-social-media-mental-health.

9. "Confidence," Psychology Today, psychologytoday.com/ca/basics/confidence.

10. Rachel Hollis, *Girl, Stop Apologizing: A Shame-Free Plan for Embracing and Achieving Your Goals* (New York: HarperCollins Leadership, 2019), 174–176.

11. Ruth Soukup, *Do It Scared: Finding the Courage to Face Your Fears, Overcome Adversity, and Create a Life You Love* (Grand Rapids: Zondervan, 2019), 69.

12. Kendra Cherry, "What is a Flow State?," Verywell Mind, verywellmind.com/what-is-flow-2794768.

13. Kristina Kuzmic, *Hold On, But Don't Hold Still: Hope and Humor from My Seriously Flawed Life* (New York: Penguin Life, 2020), 33.

NOTES

14 Amanda Laird, *Heavy Flow: Breaking the Curse of Menstruation* (Toronto: Dundurn Press, 2019), 57.

15 Anxiety Canada, "Thinking Traps," anxietycanada.com/articles/thinking-traps.

16 Thomas Oppong, "Want to Rewire Your Brain for Meaningful Life Changes? Do These Things Immediately," getpocket.com/explore/item/want-to-rewire-your-brain-for-meaningful-life-changes-do-these-things-immediately.

17 Jordan Lee Dooley, *Own Your Everyday: Overcome the Pressure to Prove and Show Up for What You Were Made to Do* (New York: WaterBrook, 2019), 55.

18 Leslie Riopel, "The Importance, Benefits, and Value of Goal Setting," PositivePsychology.com, July 12, 2021, positivepsychology.com/benefits-goal-setting.

19 Sharon Chan and Miguel Debono, "Replication of Cortisol Circadian Rhythm: New Advances in Hydrocortisone Replacement Therapy," *Therapeutic Advances in Endocrinology and Metabolism* 1, no. 3 (June 2010): 129–138, doi.org/10.1177/2042018810380214.

20 Jon Kabat-Zinn, "Exclusive Interview with Mindfulness Expert Dr. Jon Kabat-Zinn," PsychAlive, psychalive.org/video-interview-with-mindfulness-expert-dr-jon-kabat-zinn.

21 Jay Shetty, *Think Like a Monk: Train Your Mind for Peace and Purpose Every Day* (London: Thorsons, 2020), xvi.

22 Caroline Leaf, *Cleaning Up Your Mental Mess: 5 Simple, Scientifically Proven Steps to Reduce Anxiety, Stress, and Toxic Thinking* (Grand Rapids: Baker Books, 2021), 28.

23 Danny Penman, "What Exactly Is Mindfulness? It's Not What You Think," Psychology Today, January 19, 2018, psychologytoday.com/ca/blog/mindfulness-in-frantic-world/201801/what-exactly-is-mindfulness-it-s-not-what-you-think.

24 Kate Pickert, "The Art of Being Mindful," *Time*, February 3, 2014, 45.

25 Emily Nagoski and Amelia Nagoski, *Burnout: The Secret to Unlocking the Stress Cycle* (New York: Ballantine Books, 2019), 133.

26 Priya Parker, *The Art of Gathering: How We Meet and Why It Matters* (New York: Riverhead Books, 2018), xi.

27 Mary Pipher and Sara Pipher Gilliam, "The Lonely Burden of Today's Teenage Girls," *The Wall Street Journal*, August 15, 2019, wsj.com/articles/the-lonely-burden-of-todays-teenage-girls-11565883328.

28 Glennon Doyle, *Untamed* (New York: The Dial Press, 2020), 259.

29 Sophia Amoruso, *#Girlboss* (New York: Portfolio, 2015), 16.

Bibliography

Ambrosini, Melissa. *Mastering Your Mean Girl: The No-BS Guide to Silencing Your Inner Critic and Becoming Wildly Wealthy, Fabulously Healthy, and Bursting with Love*. New York: TarcherPerigee, 2016.

Amoruso, Sophia. *#Girlboss*. New York: Portfolio, 2015.

Baker, Dan, and Cameron Stauth. *What Happy People Know: How the New Science of Happiness Can Change Your Life for the Better*. New York: Rodale, 2003.

Dooley, Jordan Lee. *Own Your Everyday: Overcome the Pressure to Prove and Show Up for What You Were Made to Do*. New York: WaterBrook, 2019.

Doyle, Glennon. *Untamed*. New York: The Dial Press, 2020.

Forleo, Marie. "Authenticity." Chap. 3 in *Everything Is Figureoutable*. New York: Portfolio, 2019.

Fuligni McKay, Danielle. *Girl on Purpose*. California: MyGirl Coaching, 2018.

Hollis, Rachel. *Girl, Stop Apologizing: A Shame-Free Plan for Embracing and Achieving Your Goals*. New York: HarperCollins Leadership, 2019.

Hudson, Kate. *Pretty Happy: Healthy Ways to Love Your Body*. New York: Dey Street Books, 2016.

Kuzmic, Kristina. *Hold On, But Don't Hold Still: Hope and Humor from My Seriously Flawed Life*. New York: Penguin Life, 2020.

Laird, Amanda. *Heavy Flow: Breaking the Curse of Menstruation*. Toronto: Dundurn Press, 2019.

Leaf, Caroline. *Cleaning Up Your Mental Mess: 5 Simple, Scientifically Proven Steps to Reduce Anxiety, Stress, and Toxic Thinking*. Grand Rapids: Baker Books, 2021.

Nagoski, Emily, and Amelia Nagoski. *Burnout: The Secrets to Unlocking the Stress Cycle*. New York: Ballantine Books, 2019.

Parker, Priya. *The Art of Gathering: How We Meet and Why It Matters*. New York: Riverhead Books, 2018.

Rapinoe, Megan. *One Life*. New York: Penguin Press, 2020.

Shetty, Jay. *Think Like a Monk: Train Your Mind for Peace and Purpose Every Day*. London: Thorsons, 2020.

Soukup, Ruth. *Do It Scared: Finding the Courage to Face Your Fears, Overcome Adversity, and Create a Life You Love*. Grand Rapids: Zondervan, 2019.

Strahan, Michael, and Veronica Chambers. *Wake Up Happy: The Dream Big, Win Big Guide to Transforming Your Life*. New York: Atria, 2015.

About the Author

Lindsay Sealey, MA Ed, is a dedicated educator and consultant, a passionate keynote speaker, and the author of the award-winning books *Growing Strong Girls* and *Rooted, Resilient, and Ready*. She holds a BA from Simon Fraser University on the West Coast of Canada and an MA in educational leadership from San Diego State University. She is currently pursuing mind-body lifestyle research.

Lindsay is the founder of Bold New Girls and Brave New Boys—teaching and coaching designed to empower growing minds of all ages and with diverse experiences to be healthy, happy, and confident and to become even more of who they choose to be. Lindsay is interested in the integration of personal growth and academic success.

She is enthusiastic about personal growth and enjoys learning, creating, fitness, food, adventuring, and appreciating abundant living with her partner in Vancouver, Canada. Lindsay is excited to dive into her philanthropic and advocacy passion projects.